The World's
GREATEST
MISTAKES

The World's
GREATEST
MISTAKES

Nigel Blundell

Acknowledgements

With a book such as this, covering such a wide variety of true stories, the author must draw much of his inspiration from earlier works. It would be impossible to mention even a major proportion of them, but the author wishes in particular to acknowledge the following writers.

Stephen E. Ambrose: *Crazy Horse and Custer* (Macdonald and Jane's 1976); Charles Bateson: *The War With Japan* (Cresset Press 1968); Dee Brown: *Bury My Heart At Wounded Knee, An Indian History of the American West* (Barrie and Jenkins 1970); Basil Collier: *The War in the Far East* (Heinemann 1969); Rupert Furneaux: *The Two Stranglers of Rillington Place* (1961) and *Great Clashes of the Twentieth Century* (Odhams 1970); James Gilbert: *The World's Worst Aircraft* (M. & J. Hobbs and Hodder and Stoughton 1975); Robert Gray: *A History of London* (Hutchinson 1978); Royal B. Hassrick: *The Colourful Story of the North American Indians* (Octopus 1974); James Leasor: *Singapore* (Hodder and Stoughton 1968); Walter Lord: *A Night To Remember* (Longman and Holt, Rinehart & Wilson) and *Day Of Infamy* (Longmans, Green & Co 1957); Sir Compton Mackenzie: *Gallipoli Memories* (Cassell 1929); John Michell and Robert J. M. Rickard: *Phenomena, A Book of Wonders* (Thames and Hudson 1977); Alan Moorehead: *Gallipoli* (Hamish Hamilton 1956); Piers Paul Read: *The Train Robbers* (W. H. Allen, the Alison Press and Secker and Warburg 1978); John Selby: *The Thin Red Line of Balaclava* (Hamish Hamilton 1970); Nevil Shute: *Slide Rule* (Heinemann 1954); Time Magazine: *Special report on the Mafia* (May 16, 1977); Philipp Vandenberg: *The Curse of the Pharaohs* (Hodder and Stoughton 1976).

The publishers would like to thank the following organisations and individuals for their kind permission to reproduce the photographs in this book.

Associated Newspapers Ltd., 65; Aston Martin, 29; The British Tourist Authority, 162 left; Daily Mirror Library, 21, 41; Mary Evans Picture Library, 53; Illustrated London News, 113; Keystone Press Agency, 25, 27, 32, 36 below right, 95, 97 above and below, 109, 111 below, 119, 120 above, 126, 128, 133, 138, 144, 145, 147, 162 right, 185, 186 left, 213 below right, 219, 221; Mansell Collection, 11, 15, 35, 54, 71 above and below right, 74, 114, 120 below, 173, 213; National Army Museum, 202, 205, 209; Popperfoto, 36, 43, 50, 68, 71 left, 73, 76, 83, 85, 86, 93, 101, 131, 141 above left and right and below, 154, 161, 178, 180, 182, 186 right, 187, 196, 199; Radio Times, Hulton Picture Library, 176, 206.

First published 1980 by
Octopus Books Limited
59 Grosvenor Street, London W1
ISBN 0 7064 1128 5
This edition published 1982
Reprinted 1983
© 1982 Octopus Books Ltd
Produced by Mandarin Publishers Limited
22a, Westlands Road, Quarry Bay,
Hong Kong
Printed in Hong Kong

Contents

Introduction

For every success in the history of the world, there has also been a mistake. For every breakthrough, there has been a setback. For every genius, there has been a blunderer.

The successes, of course, are well recorded for posterity. The names of the geniuses are carved on monuments and written large in history books. But what of the people who got it all wrong . . . those who, often because of one tiny slip-up, changed the course of events?

This book sets out to put the record straight. Gathered together within these covers is the greatest galaxy of mistakes, mishaps and misfortunes ever assembled.

Some are simple, humorous cases of ordinary people whose errors of judgement would otherwise be forgotten   like the priest who married the bride to the best man. Others are remarkable instances of mismanagement—like the town that alone waged war against the Soviet Union for half a century.

There are also hoaxes (like the joker who fooled the British navy) and gullibilities (like the con-man who sold off the White House and the Statue of Liberty).

Add to these the touching tales of errors that are, quite simply, human and very understandable. Like the man who lost £32 million of his firm's money, and the speck of fluff that revealed a secret royal romance.

There is also a more serious side to this book. For told here are the stories of mistakes so monumental that they have irrevocably altered the course of history. They are mistakes that have cost dearly in money, honour and human life. They include the sinking of the Titanic, the crash of the R101 airship, the assault on Gallipoli, the defence of Singapore, Custer's Last Stand and the rise of the Mafia.

Take all these incidents and a whole lot more—slip-ups, follies, mistimings and incomprehensible idiocies. What you end up with is the most astonishing miscellany of mistakes ever assembled. Some are laughable. Some are sad. But we believe that they will all prove utterly fascinating.

Chapter One

People and Places

American president, English baker, African tribeswoman, Italian explorer, the British Navy, Australian, Brazilian and Canadian planners – the list of those who have made monumental mistakes is as wide ranging as it is endless. And it takes no more account of status than it does of nationality – as the following pages show.

The baker who burned down London

He left an oven alight – and sparked off the Great Fire of 1666

For a humble tradesman, John Farynor had attained a special honour and reputation. He was baker to King Charles II, recently restored to the English throne after his exile in France.

Farynor had been the royal baker for five years when, one evening in 1666, after another long and weary day, he climbed the stairs to bed above his bakery in Pudding Lane. He snuffed out his candle and settled down for a peaceful night's sleep. But as he slept, a flame still flickered in the bakery beneath. He had failed to damp down his bread ovens.

The flame grew. And at two o'clock that morning, on September 2, 1666, the fire in the bakery sparked off one of the worst conflagrations in history, the Great Fire of London.

Sparks rising from Farynor's establishment set fire to a pile of hay stacked in the courtyard of the nearby Star Inn and lit up the sky. Pudding Lane lay at the centre of an overcrowded area of old London, and thousands of the local inhabitants were soon out in the streets watching the blaze. They were not unduly alarmed. Fires were common in this city of pitch-soaked timbers and lathe-and-plaster constructions. Only the year before, King Charles had written to the Lord Mayor urging him to enforce more stringent fire regulations. But previous fires had fizzled out, and there was no reason to think that this one would be any different.

Pudding Lane was a dumping ground for offal from nearby Eastcheap Market, and no one of any note lived there. But it was close to the main road running down to London Bridge, so in the early hours of the morning the mayor was informed. When he arrived at the scene he was singularly unimpressed. 'Pish!' he said. 'A woman might piss it out.'

Diarist Samuel Pepys was no more impressed. He was awoken by his maid at 3 a.m. at his house about three-quarters of a mile to the east near Tower Hill. He wrote of the fire in his diary: 'I rose and slipped on my nightgown and went to her window and thought it to be at the backside of Mark Lane at the farthest, and so to bed again and asleep.'

Pepys carried the news of the fire to the court, and thereby to the king, when he arrived at his office in Whitehall shortly before midday. No one had

bothered to tell the king before then. It was Sunday, after all.

But any idea that the fire would fizzle out was soon dispelled. On Sunday afternoon the blaze reached the River Thames, and warehouses loaded with timber, oil, brandy and coal exploded like bombs, one after another.

A steady dry wind blew continuously from the east, so that, although the fire barely reached Pepys's house a short distance away, it spread uncontrollably to the west. There was one stage on the Sunday when the blaze might have been halted. But the fire-fighters smashed up the water pipes to fill their buckets more quickly and cut off the area's water supply.

The inferno swept on unabated from Sunday to Wednesday. By then, 13,000 houses had been destroyed, 87 parish churches burned down and 300 acres blackened. The shops built on London Bridge caught fire. Sparks carried across to the opposite bank of the Thames and started small fires in Southwark. The Guildhall and the Royal Exchange – the city's financial centre – were reduced to ashes.

The greatest conflagration was at St. Paul's Cathedral, where the heat caused the stonework to explode and ancient tombs to burst open, revealing mummified remains. The cathedral's roof melted, and molten lead flooded down neighbouring streets.

Remarkably, only eight people died in the Great Fire of London. Most citizens had plenty of time to flee. The roads were crammed with handcarts piled with belongings, and the surrounding countryside was one vast refugee camp.

Pepys was among those who left the city. He wrote, 'With one's face in the wind, you were almost burned with a shower of fire drops [from this] most horrid, malicious, bloody flame . . . [above it all was] a smoke so great as darkened the sun at midday. If at any time the sun peeped forth it looked red like blood.'

By Wednesday night the fire had been virtually contained, largely due to the personal intervention of the king, who organised the fire-fighters in knocking down buildings to clear a fire-break. But London smouldered for weeks afterwards. Cellars were still burning six months later.

Baker Farynor's blunder did result in some good, however. The shameful slums of central London were wiped out in a single week. And the fire purged the last vestiges of London's previous disaster, the Great Plague of 1665, which had claimed 100,000 victims.

Files of documents on pending trials were found stacked in a public lavatory in Rome Law Courts when lawyers invited newsmen to see the Italian legal system in action.

A woman was pronounced dead by a doctor after she was found frozen stiff in her unheated caravan in 15 degrees of frost. Porters were wheeling her into the morgue at a hospital in Ontario, Canada, when they heard a faint gasp. It was the 'dead' woman, who later recovered with no ill-effects.

40 years in bed – with 'flu

A doctor taking over a local practice visited a 74-year-old woman who had been bedridden for 40 years. He could find nothing wrong with her. He discovered that one of his predecessors had ordered the woman to bed because she had influenza and had told her not to get up again until he returned. He forgot to return.

Within a few days, the 34-year-old single woman had recovered. But she remained in her sickroom awaiting the doctor's visit. Several weeks elapsed and he still did not call. By then the patient had discovered that she enjoyed being waited on hand and foot – and she refused to budge.

At first, she was nursed by her mother. But when the old woman died, a brother-in-law took over. Finally, a new doctor to the area paid a routine call to the patient's home in Taunton, Devon, and examined the woman, now aged 74 and still keeping resolutely to her bed. He referred her case to a geriatrics specialist.

The specialist, Dr. Peter Rowe, said: 'By the time I saw her, she couldn't have got up if she had wanted to. She was decidedly plump and far from keen to leave her bed.'

Dr. Rowe reported the case to British medical journals in 1978, but, because of medical ethics, the woman's name was never revealed. The doctor told how it took seven months of sympathetic encouragement before the old lady was persuaded to leave her bed; and how, happily, she took to her feet again for three 'fairly active' years before her death at 77.

STERILITY MAY BE INHERITED.
– Pacific Rural Press

East is West

Columbus died without knowing he had discovered America

A light breeze filled the sails of the three tiny wooden-hulled ships and gently wafted them out of the bustling port of Palos, on Spain's southern coast. The date was Friday, August 3, 1492.

There was more than a little apprehension among the 87 men on board. This was to be a voyage of discovery – beyond the horizon of the known world. Ahead lay the Atlantic Ocean, mighty and mysterious.

But for one man watching the coast slipping slowly out of sight from the 70-foot-long flagship *Santa Maria*, the thought of sailing into the unknown held no terror.

Captain Christopher Columbus – born in about 1445 Cristoforo Columbo, the son of a Genoese clothmaker – was a proud, stubborn, ambitious mariner who dreamed of opening up a new sea route from Spain to the rich spice isles of the East Indies. For years, while sailing the shipping lanes around Portugal and Spain and down the coast of Africa to the Canary Islands, he had been planning an Atlantic crossing.

Columbus was convinced the world was round, an unpopular theory in his day, but one that was gaining support. He believed the eastern coast of Asia and the gold-rich lands of the Orient lay west of Europe, within easy sailing distance.

Now at last he was on his way, under the patronage of Spain's King Ferdinand and Queen Isabella. (His first projected attempt had been turned down eight years before by Portugal's John II.) He was about to make perhaps the biggest blunder of any explorer – but, in doing so, he was also to make the greatest discovery.

He headed his ships for San Sebastian in the Canaries, then, on September 6, eager not to miss the prevailing easterly winds, he turned the small fleet west into the open Atlantic. The square-rigged ships made good progress in the following wind. But by the middle of the month, with land still not in sight, his men became worried. They feared they might never be able to return to Spain.

Columbus, too, must have begun to doubt his estimate of the distance to the Indies. On September 19, he began to keep a false log, in which he sought to allay the fears of his crew by underestimating the miles he was sailing.

Together the *Santa Maria*, with her attendant vessels, the *Pinta* and *Nina*,

rode out the perils of the Sargasso Sea, sometimes battered by high seas, at other times becalmed for days. Columbus, desperate for his expedition to succeed and mindful of the rewards that would be heaped on him by a grateful king and queen, clutched at any evidence that they were nearing land. Hopes were often raised and dashed.

Then, at two o'clock on the morning of October 2, just 37 days after they had left the Canaries, a seaman on board the *Pinta* raised the cry: 'Land!' Later that day, the small fleet hove to off an island which Columbus named San Salvador.

Columbus wrote in his log that day: 'There we soon saw naked natives ... A landscape was revealed to our eyes with lush green trees, many streams and fruits of various types.' The next day he wrote: 'I saw that some of the men had pierced their noses and had put a piece of gold through it ... By signs, I could understand that we had to go to the south to meet a king who had great vessels of gold.'

On October 17 he noted: 'On all these days I have been in India it has rained more or less ...' He still firmly believed that he had made his landfall on the eastern coast of Asia.

Columbus set about exploring, and sailed among the Caribbean islands to the north coast of Cuba, and on to Hispaniola. He was much impressed by what he saw and in his log of October 28, while off the Cuban coast, he wrote: 'I dare to suppose that the mighty ships of the Grand Khan come here and that from here to the mainland is a journey of only ten days.'

After eight months at sea, Columbus returned in triumph to Spain where he was made 'Admiral of the ocean sea and governor of the islands newly discovered in the Indies'. He made four voyages of discovery to Central America in the next ten years, and only towards the end of his explorations did he begin to doubt whether he had in fact found the eastern coast of Asia.

It was on his third voyage to the New World, in 1498, that he began to reflect on the possibility that he had found a new continent. A more southerly course across the Atlantic had led him to the island of Trinidad, and, while exploring in the nearby Gulf of Paria, he came to the place where the mighty Orinoco River of South America flows into the sea. In his log of August 14,

---

In reference A, the cover letter at Reference B is an error. The additions at Annex B to Reference B are already incorporated in Annex A to Reference B, and are those additional items per pack that will be required if the complete schedule at Annex A to Reference B are approved.
– British Defence Ministry publication

1498, he wrote: 'I believe that this is a very large continent which until now has remained unknown.'

In the next few years, Italian adventurer Amerigo Vespucci and others were to confirm his suspicions. Vespucci explored much of Brazil's coastline, and it was the accounts of his discoveries that eventually won him the honour of having the great new continent named after him.

But in 1502, when Columbus set out on his fourth voyage, he still believed that the islands he had discovered on his first two voyages were off the eastern coast of Asia. He reasoned that a passage through to Asia must exist between these islands and the great new land to the south. So he set out to find it. And for the second time he stumbled across America without really knowing it.

For nine months, in gruelling weather, he explored along the coasts of Honduras, Costa Rica and Panama. Then, in May 1503, with his storm-battered ships worm-eaten, leaking and in danger of sinking, he struck north in a desperate bid to reach the new Spanish settlement of Santo Domingo, on the island of Hispaniola. He failed, and spent 12 months as a castaway on Jamaica before being rescued with his crew and taken back to Spain.

Columbus died on May 20, 1506. He was never to know that the land he had discovered was in fact the vast continent of America.

The prophetess who led her tribe to death

Nongqawuse had a fatal charisma. She was so smooth-tongued that she led an entire South African tribe to obliteration. And she was just 14 years old.

One hot, still day in 1856 she sat on a rock overlooking a pool in the Gxara River and, as she stared at the placid water, she imagined she saw faces reflected there.

She ran back to her village and told the elders of her tribe, the Gcaleka Xhosas, that she had seen the faces of her ancestors and that they had spoken to her. They had told her that they were ready to be resurrected to lead a holy war against the Europeans who were taking over their country.

But, said, Nongqawuse, the ancestors would only return to earth at a price. The tribe would first have to prove their faith by destroying all their worldly wealth. They would have to burn their crops and slaughter all their

> The evening of clairvoyance on Tuesday December 4 at 7 p.m. has been cancelled owing to unforeseen circumstances.
> — *East Kent Times*

cattle – otherwise they would be turned into reptiles and insects and destroyed in a tempest.

February 18, 1857, was the appointed day on which the ancestral dead would be reborn to fight again. The Gcaleka Xhosas met the deadline. They spent almost a year taking part in a prolonged orgy of ceremonial massacre and destruction.

Eventually the great day arrived. The hungry tribesfolk rose early for fear of missing the promised miracle. Nongqawuse told them to watch the sun rise and to chart its progress across the sky. It would, she predicted, halt in the heavens – then retrace its course to set for the first time in the east.

Throughout the day, the sun continued on its inevitable course. Tribespeople, half blinded through staring at it, wailed in despair. And, as the sun died in the west, their despair turned to anger. Even hungrier than they had been at dawn, they peered around for the young prophetess – but she had fled.

Nongqawuse sought sanctuary with the British in King William's Town. They placed her, for her own protection, on Robben Island. Later she moved secretly to Eastern Province, where she lived on a farm until her death in 1898.

The tribe she had led to ruin were not so lucky. They had no food, nor the means of providing themselves with any. Though many were helped by neighbouring tribes and European charity, 25,000 died of starvation.

Just one of those days

Joe Ramirez, 19 years of age, drove to the court house in a New York suburb to face a traffic charge. As his case was about to be called he realised that his parking meter was running out, so he asked the judge for time to feed it. His request was granted.

Joe raced out and was starting across the street when a policeman grabbed him for jay-walking. He gave Joe a ticket – and a long lecture. So long a lecture that a traffic warden got to his car first and gave him a ticket.

When he got back to court, the judge had gone to lunch. Joe had to feed the meter until he returned. He was duly fined $5, as he had expected, but when he took out his wallet to pay, he found that his parking fees had left him with only $2. The court clerk accepted the money on a promise that the remainder would be forthcoming and Joe, now broke, walked two miles home.

When he arrived at his house, he found a letter on the mat. It read: 'Please report for induction in the U.S. Army. . . .'

The golf club that sold its own course

The Royal Melbourne is one of the most exclusive golf courses in the world. Australia's rich and famous, as well as many international stars, have played there. But for one disastrous week, it was uncertain whether there would ever again be a Royal Melbourne to play on.

The crisis occurred at the start of the 1978 Australian PGA Championship. Stars like Johnny Miller and Severiano Ballesteros were competing on the immaculately manicured 18 holes when the club committee made the greatest golfing blunder of all time. They sold almost a third of the course from under the golfers' feet.

The club had planned to make extra cash for improvements by selling one acre of wasteland to a local house-builder. Instead, they got their plans mixed up and sold him the 8th, 9th, 10th and 11th fairways.

The builder, Mike Warson, discovered the mistake only when he was refused planning permission to subdivide the acre he thought he had bought. 'My surveyor checked up and found that the club had signed away 60 acres,' he said.

The land that the club had inadvertently sold was worth almost $20 million – a hundred times more than Warson had paid for it. He said: 'It's quite a bargain, even if you don't know what a five-iron looks like. We all had a good laugh at the club's expense.'

But as the championship continued, Warson decided to help the club out of the bunker it had landed itself in. He returned the land.

> A golfer at Livermore, California, sent a ball through the window of an aircraft landing at the local airport. It struck the pilot on the head but the plane landed safely.

The cowboy yarn written by computer

Computer expert Gilbert Bohuslav was so proud of his brainiest 'baby', a computer named DEC 11/70, that he thought he could teach it to write a Western story.

DEC 11/70 is the most advanced computer in its class at Brazosport College, Houston, Texas. It had already proved itself a master at playing chess with Bohuslav, so the young computer engineer fed into it some new information – all the most-used words in every Western movie he had ever seen.

DEC started shooting out its Wild West yarn, and with it shot down the Bohuslav Kid's theory. For this is the story that DEC told:

'Tex Doe, the marshal of Harry City, rode into town. He sat hungrily in the saddle, ready for trouble. He knew that his sexy enemy, Alphonse the Kid, was in town.

'The Kid was in love with Texas Horse Marion. Suddenly the Kid came out of the upended Nugget Saloon. "Draw, Tex," he yelled madly. Tex reached for his girl, but before he could get it out of his car, the Kid fired, hitting Tex in the elephant and the tundra.

'As Tex fell, he pulled out his own chess board and shot the Kid 35 times in the King. The Kid dropped in a pool of whisky. "Aha," Tex said, "I hated to do it but he was on the wrong side of the Queen." '

Bohuslav gave up his experiment and went back to playing chess.

Politician Horatio Bottomley backed the wrong horse when he attempted to clean up on a race in Belgium. In fact, he backed several wrong horses.

Bottomley, who owned an English racing stable, tried to beat the bookies by entering his six best horses for one minor race at Blankenberg. He then bet varying amounts on every horse and ordered his jockeys to race home in a particular order.

Unfortunately for Bottomley, a thick sea mist blew in over the lengthy coastal racecourse, causing the leading jockeys to lose touch with one another. The plotting politician watched horrified as his horses straggled past the finishing post in a hopelessly unplanned order – losing him a small fortune.

Excuse me ... I've just jumped off the Empire State Building

A young artist, broke and alone in New York during Christmas 1977, decided to kill himself. He took a lift to the 86th floor of the Empire State Building.

For a few moments, John Helms, aged 26, clung to the safety fence around the observation floor. He said a short prayer. Then he launched himself towards the specks of cars moving along Fifth Avenue, more than 1,000 feet below.

He awoke half an hour later and found himself on a 2½-foot-wide ledge on the 85th floor, where strong winds had blown him. The unsuccessful artist decided that his prayer had been answered and gave up the idea of committing suicide.

He knocked on a window of the offices of a television station and crawled in to safety. Bill Steckman, who was working there at the time, said: 'I couldn't believe it. You don't see a lot of guys coming in through the window of the 85th floor. I poured myself a stiff drink. . . .'

Helms himself found that Christmas was not such a bad time to be alive, after all. Hundreds of families called him to offer him a home for the holidays.

During a parade through Ventura, California, a drum major twirled his baton and threw it high into the air.

It hit a power cable and melted. It also blacked out ten blocks, put a radio station off the air and started a grass fire.

Washington's diplomatic disasters

What the White House aide said to the ambassador's wife

The setting was magnificent – a Washington diplomatic dinner party. VIP guests from all corners of the globe were there, the men resplendent in tuxedos, the women dripping with jewels.

Then a young, bright, handsome man, one of President Carter's senior aides, perpetrated one of the most talked-about diplomatic gaffes of the century. Apparently somewhat the worse for the fine wine being served, he undid the top button of his shirt and loosened his tie; then, according to guests, his eyes lighted upon the intriguing cleavage of attractive Mrs. Ashraf Ghorbal, wife of the Egyptian ambassador and one of the guests of honour, and he reached across as if to pull at the lady's elasticated bodice, saying: 'I've always wanted to see the pyramids.'

Few of the party guests appeared to see the joke, and moments later he stood up and announced to the company that he was off to the lavatory 'for a pee'.

The story was reported around the globe, and an embarrassed aide was able to read all about it in the international press when he awoke the following morning.

But he was not the first diplomat who had tried to foster international relations in an off-beat way and failed. One famous statesman, noted for his fondness for women, is said to have propositioned the wife of a French ambassador at an important banquet. She proved herself more diplomatic than he. Her reply: 'Not before the soup course, please, Monsieur.'

A British diplomat, addressing a Latin American leader at a public function, gesticulated with his arms to make a point. Unfortunately, his flourish dislodged the wig of his host's wife. The lady was completely bald.

Another Briton, attending the funeral of an African dignitary, was suddenly afflicted by a noisy attack of hiccups. After a moment of embarrassment, he found a way out – he forced his shoulders to heave, his face to crease and tears to pour down his cheeks. The hiccups had turned into diplomatic sobs.

One expert on protocol who prefers plain-speaking to diplomatic waffle is the Duke of Edinburgh. But he slipped up badly when he visited Kenya for its independence celebrations. The Union Jack was just about to be lowered for the last time when Prince Philip leaned over to President Jomo Kenyatta and said: 'Are you sure you want to go through with this?' Unfortunately, the microphones on the official rostrum were still switched on – and the attentive throng heard every word.

A similar fate befell America's President Jimmy Carter when he visited India. After a long meeting with his host, Premier Morarji Desai, the two men appeared before reporters and smilingly gave the diplomatic verdict that the talks had been extremely friendly.

In fact, the two leaders had argued angrily over plans for American nuclear aid to the sub-continent. And afterwards Carter whispered some very un-friendly comments about Desai to Secretary of State Cyrus Vance, who was standing beside him. What Carter forgot was that every word he said was being tape-recorded by television men invited along by the White House. The tapes were later played to an incredulous press corps. They heard the President whisper that he 'hadn't made much of an impression' on the Indian leader. And he said: 'When we get back I think we ought to write him another letter – just cold and very blunt.'

But perhaps the most public diplomatic brick was dropped only a few days earlier when the U.S. President visited Poland. Carter stepped off his jet at Warsaw airport and made a speech to the waiting crowd of 500 VIPs and officials. In English, the President's speech was friendly enough. But, as his interpreter translated it to the crowd, they became first amused, then insulted and finally furious. For the State Department interpreter spoke in a strange mixture of archaic, ungrammatical Polish, spiced with Russian. On top of that, he translated the President's warm and flattering greeting as if it were a sexual turn-on.

Carter opened his speech by saying: 'When I left the United States . . .' It was translated as: 'When I abandoned the United States.' The interpreter then quoted his leader as saying that the Polish Constitution was 'a subject of ridicule'. 'Our nation was founded' came out as 'Our nation was woven'.

Carter tried to tell the Poles: 'I understand your hopes for the future.'

> **Soon after his election, American President Calvin Coolidge invited a party of country friends to dine at the White House. Feeling rather self-conscious in such opulent surroundings, they copied Coolidge's every move. As the President poured half his coffee into his saucer, so did they. He added cream and sugar, and they did likewise. The President then laid his saucer on the floor for his cat.**

The interpreter told them: 'I know your lust for the future.' The final straw was when Carter's 'I have come to learn your opinions and understand your desires for the future,' became: 'I desire the Poles carnally.'

At that moment, as the Poles fumed, giggled or scratched their heads, the promising diplomatic career of one interpreter appeared to have come to an abrupt end.

Driver saved a toll fare, and 170 died

The tragedy of the Spanish seaside campsite of Los Alfaques was a disaster that should never have happened. In July 1978 an eight-wheel tanker hauling pressurised liquid gas south from a refinery at Tarragona exploded as it passed along the coast road near the town of Tortosa. The tanker roared through the camp's perimeter wall and flung blazing gas over a quarter-mile radius. A 200-foot ball of fire incinerated tents and caravans as it swept through the camp towards the beach. The blast flung holidaymakers over the sand and into the Mediterranean. More than 170 people died, 20 of them children.

So terrible was the devastation that the bodies were unidentifiable, metal was melted and the earth was blackened. Men were indistinguishable from women.

In the aftermath of the tragedy, stunned locals protested that they had been complaining for months about tanker drivers who were using the busy urban coast road rather than pay the toll on a nearby expressway.

The cost of saving those 170 lives would have been 1,000 pesetas – just £7.

A quarter of a million demonstrators gathered in Washington in 1978 to celebrate Sun Day, in support of non-polluting solar energy. They left behind ten acres of ankle-deep litter.

Through the roof

Opera house costs soared by £55 million

Australia's Sydney Opera House is awe-inspiring – a beautiful, soaring, shell-like edifice standing on a peninsula that juts into the city's magnificent harbour.

Sydneysiders agree that it is worth every penny of the £5 million it was estimated that it would cost. Unfortunately, the estimate was a bit out – £55 million out, give or take a million or so.

For not only is the Sydney Opera House the biggest modern building in the world, but it also turned out to be the most expensive, the most difficult to construct and the longest to complete.

The design of the Opera House began as rough drawings made in the early 1950s by Danish architect Jorn Utzon, who conceived the idea while gazing at Elsinore Castle, the setting of Shakespeare's *Hamlet*. Utzon submitted his ideas when the New South Wales government ran an international competition for the best plans for their prestigious cultural showpiece. He won and moved to Australia to launch the project, which eventually got under way in March 1959.

It did not take long for Utzon to discover that his original concept, grandiose as it was, did not work. For a start, the architect had planned the ten massive shells of the roof as thin skins of self-supporting concrete, but, since they were up to 200 feet high, the shells had to be supported by hefty arches. The re-designing of the roof made it the heaviest in the world – 26,000 tons, not including the million white tiles needed to face it.

As costs zoomed, so did the blood pressure of the New South Wales leaders. They launched lotteries with enormous prizes to help pay the bills for their white elephant. Plans were trimmed back so that, in size and seating, the auditoriums did not match those of opera houses already existing. There were

25

stories of walls being built, then pulled down again so that workmen could move their equipment from one part of the building to another.

A tough Minister of Works, David Hughes, was ordered to devote himself virtually full-time to the Opera House project. He and the architect clashed bitterly and publicly. Utzon resisted alterations pushed through by Hughes and claimed that the minister was spoiling the work already done. He said Hughes had wasted more than £15 million and lost over two or three years' work by pulling down and rebuilding parts of the structure. Hughes replied that Utzon had described the Opera House as a symphony – 'and if he had had his way it would remain an unfinished symphony'.

In 1966, Utzon left Australia. He complained that he had not been responsible for any of the original estimates on which the project had been given the go-ahead and said that they had always been unrealistic.

The project continued under a consortium of Australian architects who got to grips with the problems of the interior, which in four-and-a-half acres had to accommodate an opera and ballet theatre, a concert hall, a recording theatre, a cinema, and numerous restaurants and public rooms.

The fate of the operatic auditorium was sealed when the Australian Broadcasting Commission won the right to run the biggest hall, which had originally been earmarked for opera. So operatic and ballet performances were banished to the smaller theatre, which holds only 1,500 people – 1,300 fewer than the theatre from which the resident Sydney company were waiting to move.

As opening date approached, more problems cropped up. No car parks were considered until it was too late to fit them in. Plans for an underground car area beneath a nearby public park had to be dropped when construction workers refused to pull down two ancient trees on the historic site where Aborigines had performed the first native dance for British settlers in 1811. Because they had nowhere to park, members of the Sydney Symphony Orchestra threatened not to play. They said they did not fancy hauling their

Lew Grade, later to become international film and TV magnate Lord Grade, once visited a London theatre and saw a double-act which he considered a winner. He rushed backstage after the show, congratulated the performers and promised to make them big stars if they would sign up with him as their agent. He promised to double the money they were then getting.

The two performers were most enthusiastic about the offer, so Grade asked them: 'Who's your agent at the moment?' They replied: 'Lew Grade.'

Danish architect, Jorn Utzon, and the Sydney Opera House.

instruments through the streets of the city in full evening dress. They also inquired how they could be expected to get their 75 players into an orchestra pit that had been designed to seat only 60.

The ballet company complained that off-stage facilities were a joke. The lack of space at the side of the opera stage meant that if a ballet dancer took a flying leap he would flatten himself against a brick wall.

Front-of-house managers expressed doubts about the performances ever starting on time. They said that, since access roads had not been completed, theatregoers who had the foresight to journey by taxi instead of their own car would never get through the roadworks and would arrive spattered with mud after tramping through potholes.

Many artists complained about the lack of facilities for rehearsals and the absence of changing rooms. They even complained about the toilets, which they said either did not work or collapsed underneath them. But last-minute repairs were made and eventually a local newspaper reported: 'It's all cisterns go'.

The Sydney Opera House was opened by the Queen in October 1973. Opera lovers and concertgoers from all parts of Australia, along with dignitaries and guests invited from around the world, all left the amazing building later that night with praise for the awe-inspiring concept that, despite all the odds, had at last been proved a success – for the building had impressed almost everyone who had seen it.

But on that balmy, glittering night in 1973, one voice was not heard. As a final gesture of goodwill by the New South Wales government, the VIP invitation list had included Jorn Utzon. He did not attend.

When the bride married the best man

One day in the early 1920s, in Ireland, best man Albert Muldoon walked up to the altar with the bridegroom in the tiny church at Kileter, County Tyrone. But instead of standing to the right of the groom, Albert stood on his left.

The bride arrived and the ceremony began. The priest, seeing Albert standing on the left, put all his questions to him – and Albert answered them. The priest continued to the end of the ceremony and then invited the happy couple to sign the register. The slip-up only came to light when the true bride-groom insisted on signing after the priest had asked Albert to do so.

A second ceremony was immediately held – this time with Albert standing on the right.

Albert said afterwards: 'My pal Christopher, the bridegroom, was so ner-vous that he didn't seem able to speak, so I thought I had better answer for him.'

The mile-an-hour 'super-car'

The world's press was lined up to witness the delivery of the first of a new range of supercars. The £32,000, 140-mile-an-hour Aston Martin Lagonda was about to be handed over to the Marchioness of Tavistock at her home, Woburn Abbey. The Marchioness had bought the car with her Diners Club credit card as a seventeenth-wedding anniversary present for her husband, the Marquess, son of the Duke of Bedford, owner of the Abbey; and she had invited press and television to record the handing-over ceremony.

But the Lagonda, which had taken London's 1976 Motor Show by storm, failed to arrive with the awaited throaty roar and screech of tyres. Three months earlier, the mini-computer which was to have revolutionised the car's controls had blown up ('Someone misconnected a black wire to a red one,' said

American director Peter Sprague) and now, by the time of the ceremony, the Aston Martin technicians had failed to fix the trouble. And so the fastest speed that the 140-mph supercar achieved was when four embarrassed helpers pushed it down the driveway of Woburn Abbey at approximately one mile per hour. . . .

> **Victor Grant was saving up for a new car. It was to be a surprise, and he did not tell his wife that he had already amassed £500 and hidden it in a bundle of old clothes. Grant was out when the dustmen called at his home in Wrexham, North Wales - and his wife gave them the bundle to put on the dustcart. When he arrived home, Grant discovered the mistake and hired a mechanical digger to excavate the rubbish dump. After two days' searching, he gave up and started saving again. This time, he put his money in the bank.**

Operatic white elephant

White elephants do not come much bigger than the opera house at Manaus, in Brazil. It stands as a monument to the grandiose but impracticable dreams that made the city one of the most expensive in the world.

During the Brazilian rubber boom of 1890 to 1911, Manaus, sited near the junction of the Rivers Negro and Amazon, blossomed from a jumble of shacks to become the capital of the rubber industry and one of the most beautiful cities on earth. It boasted castles, châteaux, mosques, pallazos and Tudor-style mansions.

Almost all the materials, including the stone, were imported from Europe and paid for from the vast rubber fortunes then being amassed. Once the newly-rich tycoons had provided Manaus with street lighting, a sewage system, a floating dock, ornamental gardens and South America's first electric tramway, they looked around and wondered what else they could build.

That is when the most expensive materials of all were brought in to construct an opera house to be called the Teatro Amazonas. The beautiful building, with its elaborate murals and its dome of green, blue and gold tiles, was completed in 1896.

But, while the local authorities had spared no expense in building the opera house, they had overlooked one vital factor. There were too few customers. The auditorium seated 2,000, but the population of Manaus was less than 40,000. And the vast majority of the rough Amazon rubber men had no interest whatever in opera or the theatre.

Shortly after its opening, the opera house, on its imposing site overlooking the River Negro and the surrounding forest, was closed down and left to rot. The termites and humidity took over. Even when the giant chandelier crashed from its rotting supports, nobody did anything about it.

The building – and Manaus itself – slipped into obscurity and decay as the rubber industry declined. By 1930, the boom was no more than a memory.

In recent years, however, new industries have been introduced to the city, and the magnificent opera house, with its ornamental gardens, has been restored. The sound of music now rings out once more from its plush and pretentious interior. But this time it is not opera singers who fill the Teatro Amazonas with their music, but a local school choir who use the building for rehearsals about six times a year.

The Montreal Olympics fiasco
The Games raced away with a billion dollars

Montreal played proud host to the 1976 Olympic Games – and then faced a bill of $1 billion. That was the city's incredible debt after staging the Games – more than eight times the amount originally budgeted for.

Estimates of the cost of the billion-dollar Olympics had been so far out that, when they ended, Montreal property owners faced a Special Olympic Tax (levied in an effort to pay off the debt) for the next 20 years. The Province of Quebec shouldered the rest of the deficit and set about paying it off with extra tobacco taxes and a lottery.

When the Games finished, the main Olympic stadium and two Olympic hotels had still not been completed. Union troubles, bad weather, bad planning and bad money management were blamed.

It was thought that the spectacular facilities would pay for their own upkeep after the international athletes had all gone home. But the 10,000-seat Velo-

> **East German swimmer Sylvia Ester set a world 100-metres record of 57.9 seconds in 1967 – but officials refused to recognise it because she swam in the nude.**

drome (built at a cost of $50 million – $1 million for each registered track cyclist in Canada) could attract only 300 paying customers to its first national championships.

Other examples of extravagance were the $1½ million spent on walkie-talkie sets for security forces, $1 million rent for 33 cranes (more than the cost of buying them outright), and $½ million paid to the Montreal Symphony Orchestra and Chorus for miming to pre-recorded tapes played over the loudspeakers.

As soon as the Games ended, more than 3,700 tons of second-hand materials, ranging from boxers' bootlaces to 10,000 television sets, went on the market at knockdown prices. The unwanted debris filled warehouses the size of three football pitches, and only the Canadian Army had enough trucks to shift it all.

Quebec Sports Minister Claude Charron estimated the post-Olympic cost of running the complex at $5½ million a year, with income of only $2 million. He said: 'It is a monstrous heritage, born of outrageous expense, socially unjustified and economically unrealistic.'

The last word

Epitaph on a gravestone in a cemetery in Woolwich, London:

> **Sacred to the memory of**
>
> ## MAJOR JAMES BRUSH
>
> **who was killed by the
> accidental discharge
> of a pistol by
> his orderly
> 14th of April 1831**
>
> **Well done good and
> faithful servant**

Epitaph on a gravestone in a churchyard in Sheldon, Vermont, USA, to an unknown burglar shot while robbing a store in 1905:

> **HERE LIES**
> **A BURGLAR**
> **This stone**
> **was bought**
> **with money**
> **found**
> **on him**

The world's first driver – and crash victim

Nicholas Cugnot, French artillery officer, has three major world 'firsts' to his name. He became the first motorist when he invented and built a three-wheeled steam car in 1769. Within a few minutes of starting up, Cugnot became the world's first car-crash victim. He drove into a brick wall.

The intrepid inventor was not badly hurt and not at all disheartened. He improved the steering and the braking system on his car until it was capable of carrying four people at two miles an hour. He won a contract from the French War Ministry to build a much larger vehicle as a military carrier.

But Cugnot's road tests of his vehicles proved so dangerous to life and limb that, after several further crashes, he notched up yet another 'first' – he became the first man to be jailed for dangerous driving.

His military carrier was never put into service, and in 1804 he died in obscurity.

> Within the space of 20 minutes on the afternoon of October 15, 1966, a 75-year-old driver in McKinney, Texas, perpetrated four hit-and-run offences, drove on the wrong side of the road four times, caused six accidents, collected 10 traffic tickets and earned himself the label 'world's worst driver' in the *Guinness Book of Records*.

Hell hath no fury . . .

An airline pilot installed his mistress, a pretty stewardess, in a London flat. All was well in the love nest for a year, until the pilot, a married man, tired of his girlfriend and ordered her out.

The mistress pleaded with him to be allowed a few days to move, and he agreed. It proved a costly mistake.

The pilot went on a round-the-world flight. When he returned to the flat the girl had gone, leaving the apartment immaculately tidy. Only one thing was amiss – the telephone was off the hook.

He picked up the receiver and heard an American voice endlessly repeating the time. Before departing, the mistress had dialled the speaking clock in Washington D.C.

The cost of his broken love affair was a telephone bill for £1,200.

HMS *Dreadnought*.

The princes who never were

How a hoaxer fooled the British navy

The first anyone heard about the royal visit was a telegram from the Foreign Office in London to the Home and Atlantic Fleets lying at anchor off Weymouth, Dorset.

It was 1910, and Britain's naval might was unmatched. The greatest ship of the fleet was HMS *Dreadnought*, flagship of the Royal Navy. And it was to the *Dreadnought* that the message from the Foreign Office came. The telegram, signed by Foreign Under-Secretary Sir Charles Hardinge, ordered the ship to prepare for a visit by a group of Abyssinian princes. The

William de Vere Cole on his wedding day. *Inset* Virginia Woolf.

navy should fête them, make them feel important, and generally impress them with the invincibility of imperial power.

The officers of the *Dreadnought* set to, never suspecting that the telegram might be anything but genuine.

Meanwhile, at London's Paddington Station, an elegant man in top hat and morning suit was laying down the law to the stationmaster. He said he was Herbert Cholmondesly of the Foreign Office and he wanted a special train laid on to convey a party of Abyssinian princes to Weymouth. He wanted that train right away.

The stationmaster rushed off to prepare a VIP coach – never suspecting that Cholmondesly might be an impostor.

The 'man from the F.O.' was William Horace de Vere Cole, a wealthy young society man, practical joker extraordinary. It was he who had sent the telegram. And the four 'princes' who stepped aboard the special train at Paddington were his friends – famous novelist Virginia Woolf, judge's son Guy Ridley, sportsman Anthony Buxton and artist Duncan Grant. All had been heavily made up, bearded and robed by theatrical make-up expert Willy Clarkson. They were accompanied on their journey by an 'interpreter', Virginia Woolf's brother Adrian, and by joker Cole himself.

The group arrived at Weymouth to be greeted by a red carpet and a guard of honour. They were piped aboard the *Dreadnought*, which had been bedecked with bunting for the royal visit. Nowhere in the fleet could an Abyssinian flag be found, nor the music for the Abyssinian national anthem. Instead, worried officers ordered the hoisting of the flag of Zanzibar, and the band played that country's national anthem. No one need have worried – the 'princes' did not know the difference.

As the group inspected the fleet, they handed out visiting cards printed in Swahili and spoke in Latin with an unrecognisable accent. Everything they were shown was greeted with delighted cries of 'Bunga-bunga'.

They were shown every hospitality. In return, they tried to bestow Abyssinian military honours on some of the high-ranking officers. They asked for prayer mats at sunset. But they refused all offers of food and drink 'for religious reasons' – they had been warned by make-up man Clarkson that if they tried to eat anything their false lips would fall off.

The ruse was almost uncovered on two occasions. Firstly, when Anthony Buxton sneezed and half his moustache flew off (he stuck it back on before anyone noticed), and secondly, when the group were introduced to an officer who was related to Virginia Woolf and who also knew Cole quite well. But the officer did not see through Virginia's disguise and, extraordinarily, he showed no sign of recognition when he looked at Cole.

The royal party hastily ended their visit and, after posing for photographs, returned to London, where they revealed their outrageous hoax. The whole operation had cost Cole £4,000 – a princely sum in those days.

But Cole would pay almost any sum and go to almost any lengths for the sake of a practical joke. He once dressed as a workman and dug a huge hole in the middle of London's bustling Piccadilly. He kept an eye on his hole in the road for several days, watching the visits of numerous puzzled council officials. It was a week later before they realised they had been hoaxed and filled it in.

On another occasion, Cole was walking through Westminster with a Member of Parliament when the arch-joker bet the MP that he could beat him to the next corner, even after giving him a ten-yard start. The MP agreed, not realising that Cole had slipped his gold watch into his acquaintance's pocket. As the MP began running, Cole shouted: 'Stop thief!', and called over a policeman to search the 'fugitive's' pockets. The watch was found and the MP was whisked off to the nearest police station, where he had the unenviable task of persuading the police that they had all been taken for a ride.

But Cole's favourite practical jokes involved disguises. While an undergraduate at Cambridge University, he dressed up as the Sultan of Zanzibar and paid an 'official visit' to his own college. He was even conducted around his own quarters.

Another of his outlandish impersonations was when he arrived at a meeting of leading trade unionists and marched on to the platform to address them. The audience was expecting a speech by Britain's first Labour Prime Minister, Ramsay MacDonald, and indeed Cole, after spending hours making up before a mirror, did look exceedingly like him.

The real MacDonald, however, was 'lost' somewhere in London in a taxi driven by one of Cole's accomplices. Cole meanwhile was telling the union leaders that they should all work much harder for less pay. The speech did not go down well.

Canadian photographer Peter Duffy, assigned to cover the unveiling of a plaque at City Hall in Prince George, British Columbia, decided to liven up an otherwise dull afternoon by taping a large coloured nude photograph over the plaque, but under the covering drape. Then he stood back, camera at the ready, as the mayor performed the unveiling.

Duffy said: 'The mayor didn't see the picture at first, but when he did his mouth just hung open. Instead of the usual ripple of applause, there was absolute silence. Then I was sacked.'

The law really can be an ass

The law is a ass – a idiot.' That was the verdict of Mr. Bumble the beadle in the Charles Dickens classic, *Oliver Twist*. If Mr. Bumble had ever visited the young states of North America, he would have found his prejudices particularly well founded. For there, the legislators were busy drafting a whole new range of asinine laws.

These laws have been added to over the years. And, because of bureaucratic forgetfulness, they remain in force (although not often enforced) to this day.

Woe betide the citizen at Greene, New York, who eats peanuts and walks backwards during a concert – he faces the risk of prosecution.

Carrying fishing tackle in a cemetery is illegal at Muncie, Indiana. Slurping soup in a New Jersey restaurant is against the law. In Memphis, Tennessee, a local law demands that a woman must not drive a car unless a man walks in front with a red flag.

The good people of Milwaukee must keep their pet elephants on a leash while walking them on the public streets. In Oklahoma it is illegal to get a fish drunk or to attempt to catch whales in the state's inland waters.

Even insects have not escaped the attention of the law-makers. In Kirkland, Illinois, a law forbids bees to fly over the town.

Cafés are not supposed to sell ring-doughnuts in Lehigh, Pennsylvania. It is unlawful in Lexington, Kentucky, to carry an ice-cream cornet in your pocket.

The law-makers of yester-year really had a field day at Corvallis, Oregon. Spare a thought for a young girl wanting to buy a cup of coffee there after 6 p.m. Local laws say she must do without. Over at Lynn, Massachusetts, it is forbidden to serve coffee to babies in restaurants. And at Waterloo, Nebraska, barbers are barred from eating onions between 7 a.m. and 7 p.m.

But the prize for law-making gone mad must go to Thurston County, Washington. Officials there wanted to ensure that police and firemen who worked on Sundays did not have to be paid overtime rates. The legal experts were set to work and came up with the following solution: for the purposes of assessing pay rates, Sundays were henceforth abolished.

No person shall walk, run, stand, sit or lie on the grass in this pleasure ground.
— Byelaw of Newquay Urban Council, Cornwall

A canal goes down the drain

It was a tough job for Jack Rothwell and his workmates – dredging a busy stretch of the Chesterfield Canal, near Retford in Nottinghamshire. It had proved quite a problem, what with all the mud and rusting bicycles, prams and refrigerators. Now they were finding it impossible to shift a heavy iron chain lying on the bottom of the canal.

Finally, Jack, foreman of the gang, ordered the chain to be hooked to their dredger. Driver Kevin Bowskill started up and, with one sharp tug, the obstruction was freed. The workmen hauled in the chain, along with a large block of wood that was attached to the end of it, and knocked off for a tea-break.

While they were away, a passing policeman noticed an extraordinary whirlpool in the normally placid canal. He also noticed that the water level was falling. He rushed off to find the dredging gang. By the time they all returned, the canal had disappeared.

It was then that realisation dawned. Jack and his men had pulled out the plug of the canal. One-and-a-half miles of waterway had gone down the drain.

The plug, put there by James Brindley when he built the waterway 200 years earlier, had remained undisturbed until Jack's gang came along in the summer of 1978. Now, the millions of gallons of water that had filled the canal were all draining into the nearby River Idle. All that was left were a number of forlornly grounded holiday cruisers, complete with angry owners, the dredger itself, which was stuck firmly on the muddy bottom . . . and a plughole.

The town that stayed at war for 110 years

A simple slip-up put a British town at war with one of the mightiest nations on earth for more than a century. The long but peaceful war was between Russia and the border town of Berwick-upon-Tweed.

Over the centuries, Berwick had changed hands 13 times between Scotland and England. In 1482, it finally became part of England. But because of its special place in history, the town was traditionally referred to as a separate entity in all State documents.

At the outbreak of the Crimean War, England declared war on Czarist Russia in the name of Victoria, Queen of Great Britain, Ireland, Berwick-upon-Tweed and all British Dominions. The war ended in 1856, but, by an oversight, the Paris Peace Treaty of that year made no mention of Berwick.

And so the town remained officially at war with Russia for a further 110 years – until, in 1966, a Soviet official made a special goodwill visit to Berwick to declare peace.

The town's mayor, Councillor Robert Knox, replied: 'Please tell the Russian people that at last they can sleep peacefully in their beds.'

The Martians have landed!

Orson Welles' radio play threw America into a panic

Orson Welles directs *War of the Worlds*.

A few minutes after eight o'clock on the night of Sunday, October 30, 1938, a sombre voice interrupted a radio broadcast to warn Americans: 'Ladies and gentlemen, I have a grave announcement to make . . .'

The words that followed, beamed out in a programme networked across the United States, caused remarkable scenes of panic. For the grave announcement was that Martians had landed in North America and were sweeping all resistance before them in a series of bloody battles. The USA was being taken over by men from outer space.

THE WORLD'S GREATEST MISTAKES

The announcement was part of an off-beat radio play – but one so realistic and produced by such a genius of the theatre that most people who heard it took it for fact.

The programme had started undramatically enough. At 8 p.m. listeners heard: 'The Columbia Broadcasting System and affiliated stations present Orson Welles and his Mercury Theatre Of The Air in *War of the Worlds* by H. G. Wells.'

Then came the booming voice of Orson Welles: 'We know now that in the early years of the 20th century, this world was being watched closely by intelligences greater than man's.'

He was interrupted by a news announcer apparently reading a routine bulletin: 'Tonight's weather . . . For the next 24 hours there will not be much change in temperature. A slight atmospheric disturbance of undetermined origin is reported over Nova Scotia, causing a low-pressure area to move down rather rapidly over the north-eastern states, bringing a forecast of rain, accompanied by winds of light-gale force. Maximum temperature: 66. Minimum: 48. This weather report comes to you from the Government Weather Bureau.

'We now take you to the Meridian Room at the Hotel Park Plaza in downtown New York where you will be entertained by the music of Ramon Raquello and his orchestra.'

Nothing to cause alarm at that stage. But the atmosphere was being cleverly built up. Listeners who had tuned in from the start were already lulled into forgetfulness that what they were listening to was really a radio play.

Not that there were many listeners. After 16 Mercury Theatre shows, CBS bosses readily admitted that their dramatic series was not proving to be a major hit. Mercury Theatre had only 3 per cent of the listening audience. Most people were tuned on Sunday nights to The Charlie McCarthy Show on a rival network.

That was why Welles, worried by the ratings, was throwing everything into

Norway's King Haakon visited the BBC's London studios in order to record a broadcast to his people. The title of the programme was 'This is London', and it was to begin with a royal fanfare.

Unfortunately, the BBC Sound Library misunderstood its instructions and, instead of supplying a recording of a fanfare, produced one of a funfair.

The King's introduction went out over the air as: 'Roll up, roll up . . . all the fun of the fair . . .'

THE WORLD'S GREATEST MISTAKES

War of the Worlds. He knew that CBS would ditch his show if it did not find a big-money sponsor. And it would not get a sponsor if it did not gain more listeners.

Welles and his Mercury Theatre associates, Paul Stewart and John Houseman, had been working on the play for five days. They had rehearsed it, rewritten the script, and rehearsed again. On the Thursday night before it went on the air, the three men had listened to a tape of their work so far. They were not happy.

Welles, who had been rehearsing for another play in New York at the same time and who was almost asleep on his feet, was as glum as anyone had ever seen him. He said: 'Our only chance is to make it as realistic as possible. We'll have to throw in as many stunts as we can think of.' The team stayed up all night adding newsy-sounding snippets to the script. The next day Stewart worked on suitable sound effects – the noise of panicking crowds, gunfire and screams.

By Sunday night, the studio was littered with paper cups and food bags after a nervous eight-hour rehearsal. But at 7.59 p.m., as Welles gulped a bottle of pineapple juice before going on the air, everyone agreed that this show had a chance . . . that it would pinch listeners from Charlie McCarthy . . . that it would get the Mercury Theatre talked about.

What followed over the next 24 hours certainly got the Mercury Theatre – and Welles in particular – talked about. It also won listeners from the McCarthy show, and sooner than Welles had thought.

By chance, the McCarthy variety show had a new singer featured that Sunday night. He was an unknown. He came on at ten minutes past eight, and bored listeners began twiddling their dials to find out whether there was anything better on CBS. They joined *War of the Worlds* after all the preliminary announcements had been made. They had no inkling that a play was in progress. All they knew was that strange things were happening along the eastern seaboard. The CBS announcer was telling them so. . . .

'Ladies and gentlemen, I have a grave announcement to make. The strange object which fell at Grovers Mill, New Jersey, earlier this evening was not a meteorite. Incredible as it seems, it contained strange beings who are believed to be the vanguard of an army from the planet Mars.'

Soft music followed. A subtle touch to get people anxious, unsettled, edgy. What was going on?

The announcer broke in again. There was a nervous, panicky tone to his voice. The Martians, hideous leathery-skinned creatures, were spreading out. New Jersey police were racing to intercept them.

There was more music, more feverish announcements, chilling silences. People were glued to their sets. Neighbours had been called in to listen, too.

Relatives had been telephoned and warned. Across the whole of America, people were beginning to panic.

Then the announcer spluttered on to the air again: 'We take you now to Washington for a special broadcast on the national emergency by the Secretary of the Interior.' A solemn voice was heard urging people not to panic – but in the same breath telling them that the Martian landing was not restricted to New Jersey. Space vehicles were falling to earth all across the States. Thousands of troops and civilians had already been slaughtered by death-ray guns.

There were interviews with eye-witnesses, many parts being played by brilliant actor Joseph Cotten. The witnesses told how they had seen fiery objects land and foul creatures emerge from them, how death-rays had wiped out thousands, how the aliens were unstoppable.

One of Welles' actors impersonated the President of the United States and warned the American people against the dangers of panic. The show ended with an announcer screaming from the top of the CBS skyscraper that Manhattan was being overrun. His feverish commentary trailed off in a strangled scream.

By that time, many listeners had already left their radio sets. Those who stayed with the show to the end realised that it was all just a play. Those who did not were in a blind panic.

In New Jersey, where the Martians were first reported to have landed, the roads were jammed with cars racing for the hills. Families fled from their homes with wet towels over their heads, believing this would save them from the nauseous space gases they had been told about. Furniture and valuables were being piled into trucks and cars. The stampede had started.

The panic spread outwards. In New York, restaurants emptied. Bus terminals and taxi ranks bulged as people tried to get home to comfort their families. Wives rang around the bars trying to find husbands. And the word spread.

Sailors in the U.S. Navy were recalled to their ships in New York harbour to be ready to defend America against the Martians. From Los Angeles to

---

Czech housewife Vera Czermak was heartbroken when she learned of her husband's unfaithfulness. In a fit of depression, she hurled herself out of the window of her third-floor Prague apartment. Three floors below, Mr. Czermak was walking along the street. Mrs. Czermak landed on Mr. Czermak. Mr. Czermak died and Mrs. Czermak survived.

THE WORLD'S GREATEST MISTAKES

Boston there were reports of 'meteors'. Some impressionable people actually claimed to have seen Martians.

State reserve troopers called their HQs to volunteer for the defence of the world. In the Deep South, weeping, hysterical women prayed in the streets. Church services across the land were interrupted as people burst in to break the news to congregations. There was even one case of an attempted suicide.

The switchboards of newspapers and radio stations were jammed. But, surprisingly, there was no inkling of the panic in the CBS studios, where, with screams and announcements of martial law, Welles was bringing his production to a gruesome close. Welles and Cotten were told about the incoming phone calls, but Cotten said: 'They're just cranks.' Towards the end of the play, two policemen turned up at the back of the studio but, realising it was all just a play, they did not mention the panic to anyone and, instead, stayed to listen to the finale.

The first Welles knew of the result of his over-enthusiastic endeavours was when he left his apartment the following morning and saw his name in flickering lights on the neon newsboard of the *New York Times* building: 'Orson Welles Causes Panic.' He bought the newspapers and read the main headlines in the *New York Herald Tribune* – 'Attack from Mars in Radio Play Puts Thousands in Fear' – and in the *New York Times* – 'Radio Listeners in Panic: Many Flee Homes to Escape Gas Raid from Mars.'

Welles, already a well-known actor at the age of 24, was fiercely criticised for the unthinking action that had thrown half the USA into terror. Newspapers lambasted him for irresponsibility. There was talk of criminal action.

Dozens of people brought lawsuits against CBS; the total claim was $750,000. But all the suits were withdrawn and, far from taking Welles' show off the air, CBS bosses patted themselves on the back for having hired the most talked-about actor in America. The Mercury Theatre's ratings soared. It even found a sponsor.

Radio's biggest blunder had paid off.

Fairground customers queued up to see the amazing 'King Kong' – 23-year-old Mike Towell in an ape costume. Mike's act had been a big success in fairs around Britain. But his biggest hit came when he visited Huddersfield, Yorkshire. As he climaxed his act by bending back the bars of his cage and leaping into the audience, one frightened man picked up an iron bar and whacked him over the head. The man fled in panic and 'King Kong' was rushed to hospital to have six stitches put in his scalp.

Astronomer sets the British Isles a-jumping

The BBC has a reputation for staidness that has earned it the nickname 'Auntie Beeb'. But in fact it has played quite a few practical jokes on listeners and viewers.

Thousands of people thought there was magic in the air one morning in 1976 when astronomer Patrick Moore told BBC radio listeners that at exactly 9.47 a.m. the planet Pluto would pass behind Jupiter, producing an increased gravitational pull from the heavens.

Moore said that at that moment people would feel lighter, and he invited them to jump into the air to experience a floating sensation. That was how thousands of people across Britain came to be leaping into the air at 9.47 a.m. on that particular April Fool's Day. Hundreds of listeners rang the BBC afterwards to say that the jumping experiment had worked.

Famous BBC broadcaster Richard Dimbleby fooled thousands on another April Fool's Day, in 1957, when he showed a television documentary about the spaghetti harvest in Italy. Viewers saw the spaghetti wafting in the wind as it 'grew' from the branches of trees.

But sometimes it is the broadcasters who are hoaxed. Liverpool's Radio City once invited an Arabian VIP visiting Britain, His Serene Highness Prince Shubtill of Sharjah, to be interviewed about oil exploration in the Persian Gulf. The interview was recorded for a news bulletin, and the management of the radio station fêted the prince before he left.

But His Serene Highness was prankster Neville Duncan, a bank computer expert. And his impersonation was discovered 20 minutes too late when interviewer Peter Gould, a crossword fanatic, realised that Prince Shubtill's name was not Arabian after all, but an anagram of bull****.

There was panic in 1977 when an unknown electronics wizard broke into a peak-hour national newscast on British television and announced that beings from outer space had landed in Southern England. TV station and newspaper switchboards were jammed. The hoaxer was never discovered.

Today's weather: A depression will mope across northern areas.

– Daily Telegraph

Sold for £10 – the world's largest gold-field

O n an unrecorded date in July, 1886, a penniless prospector, George Harrison, stood with the Earth's greatest treasure at his feet. He had picked up a piece of yellowish metal. He was quite certain what this metal was – gold.

Thousands of men had blunted countless picks and spades and worn fingers to the bone during that decade in South Africa, the scene of the most frenzied gold rush of all time. Harrison, however, had simply picked up his nugget from the ground. By chance, he had stumbled on the one spot where what was to become South Africa's Main Reef reached the surface of the Witwatersrand.

Harrison, a veteran of the Australian gold rush, took the nugget to Gert Oosthuizen, the owner of the land on which he had made the find. Oosthuizen immediately wrote to President Paul Kruger. The letter, referring to Harrison by the Afrikaans version of his name, read:

Klipplaatdrif, 23rd July, 1886

Mr. S. J. P. Kruger
Dear Sir,
I let you know hereby that Mr. Sors Hariezon has been here to see me and has told me that the reef is payable and so I send him to you, then, Mr Kruger. You can talk to him yourself.

I remain your friend and
servant
G. C. Oosthuizen

It is unlikely that George Harrison met the President. But an official did see him and suggested he put down his discovery in an affidavit. He did:

My name is George Harrison and I come from the newly discovered gold-fields Kliprivier especially from a farm owned by a certain Gert Oosthuizen. I have a long experience as an Australian gold-digger and I think it a payable gold-field.

This simple statement recorded the discovery of the world's greatest gold-field. During the next 90 years the chain of gold mines based on the reef discovered by Harrison were to produce up to a million kilograms of gold each year – approximately 70 per cent of the gold production of the Western world.

Within two days of Harrison signing his affidavit, a petition had been drawn up asking that Oosthuizen's land, and a large area surrounding it, should be proclaimed a 'public goldfield'. The petitioners were convinced that gold in sizeable amounts would be discovered.

Magistrates granted the petition, and Harrison was granted 'Claim No. 19' of the gold-field. Around the claims a township was built – later to be named Johannesburg.

Despite this frenetic activity, it seemed that Harrison had little faith in the new diggings. He sold his claim for £10 and turned his back on the Witwatersrand. Most likely he tried to seek his fortune in Barberton, then the largest town in the Transvaal. Nobody knows what happened to him. It was rumoured that he was eaten by a lion.

The claim he had sold in November 1886 for £10 changed hands three months later for £59, Alfred Hepple then sold it to the Little Treasure Gold Mining Company for £1,500 and shares to the value of £150. On September 30, 1887, the Little Treasure Company sold it to the Northey Gold Mining and Exploration Company for £2,000 plus £8,000 in shares.

Harrison's claim continued to gain in value, and eventually it came to constitute the nucleus of the entire South African gold-mining industry.

Owzat! BBC man is caught out

Cricket commentator Brian Johnston is the undisputed clanger champion of British broadcasting. And he admits it.

Once, jet-lagged and describing the field from an Australian cricket pavilion, he told an audience of millions that there were 'five slips, with Neil Harvey standing with his legs apart waiting for a tickle.'

Another of his commentaries bowled listeners over when he announced: 'You have joined us at a very interesting time. Ray Illingworth is just relieving himself at the pavilion end.'

But Johnston reckons that his greatest gaffe was when he was searching for words to describe a player waiting to receive the ball. What he meant to say was: 'He's sticking out his bottom – like someone sitting on a shooting stick.' But Johnston so mixed up his syllables that what he really said was something quite unprintable. . . .

The normally unflappable veteran commentator John Snagge once announced to radio listeners glued to their sets during the final seconds of an exciting Boat Race: 'I don't know who's ahead . . . it's either Oxford or Cambridge.'

Another BBC man, Ron Pickering, who covered the athletics events at the 1976 Montreal Olympics, must have wished he had stayed at home after he had announced to millions of British television viewers: 'The big Cuban came out of the bend, opened his legs, and showed his class.'

Loving touch that revealed a royal romance

Margaret removed fluff from Townsend's uniform – and her secret was out

Princess Margaret with Peter Townsend.

The place was Westminster Abbey, the year 1953, the occasion the Coronation of Queen Elizabeth II. All eyes were on the young Elizabeth. All eyes except those of two people. One of them was the Queen's sister, Princess Margaret, whose admiring glance was directed at a man standing a couple of paces away from her. The other was an American reporter, who was watching Princess Margaret intently. What he later wrote was to change the course of royal history.

The reporter was studying Margaret because he had heard rumours of a romance between the pretty, petite princess and a man who was almost old enough to have been her father. That man was Group Captain Peter Townsend, a former Spitfire pilot and Battle of Britain hero.

Townsend, DSO, DFC and Bar, had entered Margaret's life in 1945 when she was just 14. The fighter ace, who had shot down 11 German planes, was assigned to Buckingham Palace as an equerry to her father, King George VI. The adolescent Margaret soon developed a 'crush' for the dashing ex-airman. And as the years passed, that infatuation did not dim.

At the Palace, the fun-loving Margaret always had to take second place to her more serious-minded sister Elizabeth, and in the background, she and Townsend were repeatedly thrown together.

In 1952 Townsend got divorced. The quiet and basically shy airman had, since 1941, been married to Rosemary Pawle, the daughter of a brigadier. They had two sons. Like Princess Margaret, Rosemary was a fun-loving girl; in the divorce case Townsend named a wealthy merchant banker as co-respondent. With the divorce, Townsend was free to return the love of the young princess.

One other, momentous event in 1952 sealed the fate of the two lovers. On the night of February 6, King George VI died. One of Margaret's closest friends was to say later that that was the night the princess really fell in love with her father's equerry. The King had doted upon his younger daughter, and whereas Elizabeth withstood the shock with fortitude, Margaret was bereft with grief. The pivot of her life had vanished, and she turned to Townsend, 16 years her senior, to fill the void.

Townsend was cautious by nature. He realised that the deep love he now felt for Margaret might have been fuelled by the failure of his marriage, and that Margaret's feelings might have been heightened by her father's death. But the 22-year-old princess had no such reservations about their love.

The romance became common knowledge among her family, who tried to end the relationship, and among her aristocratic friends, who did not approve of it. No one could countenance the idea of a love affair between one of the late king's trusted servants – a divorced family man nearing middle-age – and the young princess.

The couple made a pact to keep their love a secret from the public. No hint of scandal could be allowed to mar the Coronation.

Townsend, still an equerry, was there at Westminster Abbey, attending with members of the royal family. He stood, slim, tall and handsome, wearing his wartime decorations on his RAF uniform. Margaret, bejewelled and radiant, tried throughout the ceremony to avert her eyes from him. But she could not. She turned slightly and looked up at him. Then she stretched out her white-gloved hand and, without thinking, picked a piece of fluff from his uniform.

It was a small thing. But, as her hand brushed proudly across the tunic of medals, a lone reporter was watching eagle-eyed. It was the first public hint of this royal love affair.

The next day, the American newspapers told all they knew. But the British

Press held back from announcing the romance. There was even an official denial. But a fortnight later, the story could be suppressed no longer, and all of Britain knew the lovers' secret.

Townsend asked the Queen to release him from his service at the Palace. He took a post as air attaché at the British Embassy in Paris. He and Margaret poured their hearts out over the telephone, and Margaret sent long, affectionate letters to him almost daily. She still thought she could marry him, and was ready to give up her royal life and privileges to do so. But Townsend was conscious that the government, the Church of England and the Royal Family, particularly the Queen's husband, Prince Philip, were all against the liaison.

The British public felt differently. When Margaret drove through the streets of the East End of London, women shouted to her: 'Go on, marry him.'

But officialdom won. Townsend stayed away from Britain for two years. And at the end of that time, he admitted defeat. He decided he could not allow Margaret to sacrifice her birthright for his sake. When he returned to London, the couple met again several times – but only once alone. They had agreed to part for ever.

Throughout one night, Townsend sat up alone drafting a statement for Margaret to make. And on October 31, 1955, she announced to the press: 'I would like it to be known that I have decided not to marry Group Captain Peter Townsend. I have been aware that, subject to my renouncing my rights of succession, it might have been possible for me to contract a civil marriage. But, mindful of the Church's teachings that Christian marriage is indissoluble, I have resolved to put these considerations before any others.'

There was one part of the statement that Townsend had not written for her. Margaret added it herself. 'I have reached my decision entirely alone, and in doing so I have been strengthened by the unfailing support and devotion of Group Captain Peter Townsend.'

After that, Margaret launched herself into a whirl of party-going and Townsend set off to drive around the world by Land-Rover before setting up a new home in France. One of the great romances of the century was all over.

The always-so-correct British Broadcasting Corporation were severely embarrassed when news leaked out that they had paid white film extras up to five times as much as black extras during African location shooting of a documentary film series. Its title: The Fight Against Slavery.

Captain Cook speared to death by natives in Hawaii, 1777.

How paradise was lost

The travellers who destroyed the Island of Love

Try to imagine the nearest thing to paradise on earth and you might well think of Tahiti. For this tiny dot in the vast emptiness of the Pacific has been praised by travellers through the ages as the most beautiful place in the world.

Approach Tahiti on the deck of a ship and the island appears out of the ocean like a vision from fairyland. It is only 35 miles long yet it is capped by a 7,000-ft mountain with majestic pinnacles soaring into a ring of cloud. The slopes of the mountain glitter with streams that rush through the tropical forests clinging to its sides.

Surrounding the mountain is a flat shoreline encompassed by coral rocks, grey volcanic sand and crashing surf. Beside the island's single bumpy road are dotted huts whose woven palm walls shift noiselessly in the light breeze.

53

Captain Bligh's *Bounty*.

Today there is also the port of Papeete, with pretty white yachts, and white holidaymakers strolling around the harbour. But 200 years ago there was no port, no white people – only what early navigators described as 'the second Garden of Eden'.

The Tahitians lived an idyllic life. They were bronzed and beautiful and sensual. Love was unhidden, natural and shared. Diarists among the first explorers have recorded that the men were tall with shining teeth and perfect skins, except for the tattoos with which they adorned themselves. And the women were perfect, especially to the eyes of the sailors who had been months at sea without seeing a female form. These women wore brightly coloured, loosely fitting dresses which displayed their charms almost completely. They often went bare-breasted and generally wore flowers in their long dark hair.

Flowers – hibiscus, frangipani and jasmine – adorned the island generously. There was fruit in abundance, too, particularly coconuts and breadfruit. And in the sea there was fish for the taking. The 40,000 islanders who lived on Tahiti two centuries ago did not have to work hard for a living. Food and fresh water was provided by nature. The climate was constant. There was little sickness. No danger. Love was what life was all about. By any standards, Tahiti was indeed paradise.

Then came the white man. On April 13, 1769, Captain James Cook sailed his ship *Endeavour* into Matavai Bay, near Papeete, and dropped anchor.

His crew were not the first white men to visit Tahiti. Louis Antoine de Bougainville, in *La Boudeuse*, had put in for provisions the year before, and the Royal Navy's Captain Wallis, commanding the *Dolphin*, had called in 1767. But Bougainville had barely set foot ashore and Wallis stayed hardly a month, most of the time confined to his sickbed. Cook's longer stay, and his return to the island, were to change Tahiti for ever.

Cook was an adventurer of thirty-nine, a tough Yorkshireman from a poor background who had begun his sea career as Able Seaman Cook in the Royal Navy. He made his name as a navigator by charting Newfoundland and, against all expectations, was given a commission and put in charge of the *Endeavour* with orders to carry out astronomical surveys on Tahiti and then head south to seek the fabled 'Southern Continent'.

He arrived in Matavai Bay with ninety men, most notable of whom was a wealthy young amateur botanist, Joseph Banks, who had contributed largely to the cost of the expedition. On his return to England, he was to be lauded by society, lionised to a greater degree than Captain Cook, and eventually become president of the Royal Society, an honour he held until his death.

When the *Endeavour* dropped anchor, she must have seemed a mighty vessel to the Tahitians, used only to their outrigger canoes. But by Royal Navy standards, she was not so impressive – a 350-ton converted collier, just a hundred feet long and carrying twelve guns. The *Endeavour* had sailed from Plymouth eight months previously and the men aboard were ravenous – for fresh food, excitement and women. They had heard of the legendary beauty of the Tahitian girls and they peered expectantly shorewards as the islanders' canoes came out of Matavai Bay to inspect them. They were happy to heed Cook's final instructions before anchoring: 'Endeavour by all fair means to cultivate a friendship with the natives and treat them with all imaginable humanity.'

The Tahitians were shy at first and meekly offered palm fronds as a sign of peace. But they soon became more confident and invited the strangers to visit their homes. Joseph Banks was awed by the beauty of the place. He wrote: 'The scene we saw was the truest picture of Arcadia, of which we were going to be kings, that the imagination can form.'

Cook's first job was to set up a camp ashore, where he could prepare his instruments for the astronomical observations, most importantly the transit of Venus across the Sun due to occur on June 3. But arrangements were hampered by the islanders' petty pilfering. A constant guard had to be kept on the ship; otherwise the Tahitians would clamber aboard from canoes and steal virtually anything not fastened down. While dining ashore with a chieftain and his family, Banks had a telescope and a snuff box stolen. And Cook lost a valuable quadrant, later recovered. But most serious of all, a band of Tahitians seized a musket from one of the camp guards, who opened fire on them.

In his log, Cook glossed over the incident. But Sydney Parkinson, an artist brought along by Banks to draw the plants of the island, later put the incident in its true perspective. He wrote of the guards' reaction to the order to fire: 'They obeyed with the greatest glee imaginable, as if they had been shooting at wild ducks. They killed one man and wounded many others.' And he added: 'What a pity that such brutality should be exercised by civilised people against unarmed ignorant Indians. The natives fled into the woods like frightened fawns. They were terrified to the last degree.'

The first cracks had appeared in paradise.

The second blow fell a week later. A chieftain who had become particularly friendly with the Englishmen complained that the *Endeavour*'s butcher had threatened his wife. Cook had the butcher lashed to the rigging and invited the chief and his family on board to witness the culprit's punishment – a thrashing with the cat o'nine tails. The Tahitians wept openly and pleaded with the captain to free the man. But Cook refused, and the punishment went ahead – to the accompaniment of wails from the chief and his family. The islanders were learning the meaning of white man's justice.

What particularly bewildered the Tahitians, however, was the visitors' attitude to love-making. Among the islanders, the act was as natural as eating and was often carried out in the open, particularly among the young, who might be only 11 or 12. The Tahitians could never understand why the English sailors wanted to creep away with the women into the woods. What were they ashamed of?

At first, love on the island was offered to the white men absolutely free. Native girls would make their intentions very obvious, even to the guards on duty around the camp. The sailors and marines from the *Endeavour* availed themselves of the maidens' charms at every opportunity. So too, it is believed, did most of the officers and scientists aboard, with the exception of Cook.

But the recent visits by the ships of Wallis and Bougainville had left on the islanders the first stain of the civilised world – venereal disease. By the time the *Endeavour* left Tahiti – three months after its arrival – half the ship's company were afflicted. Also, by that time love on Tahiti was no longer free. At first, the price was an iron nail. Then two nails. Then a handful. Eventually, crewmen had to be punished for using up the ship's badly needed store of this item.

Just before the ship was due to sail, two men deserted and headed for the hills with native girls. They were recaptured and given the lash.

The *Endeavour* sailed south for Australia and Antarctica on July 13, the slow old collier being accompanied out to sea by canoes filled with waving and weeping natives. Waving back from the ship were a Tahitian chief and his servant who had begged Cook to take them with him. But they were not to survive the two-year voyage. Neither were 32 of the crew, who died of white man's diseases the *Endeavour* had carried around the world.

Cook made two further voyages to the Pacific. In August 1773 he sailed into Matavai Bay in command of another converted collier, the *Resolution*, with a crew of 117. He was accompanied by the slightly smaller *Adventurer*, with 83 men, commanded by Lieutenant Tobias Furneaux, who had sailed on the original Tahitian expedition with Wallis. Cook and Furneaux stayed only 16 days before heading south again to explore Antarctica and New Zealand. They returned to Tahiti in April 1774 and this time remained for six weeks.

Relaxing after the rigours of Antarctica and with no vital duties to perform

He said: 'I was playing my recording of the *Messiah* when Mrs. X said that this was not the time for music. She then made overtures to me.'

– *News of the World*

on the island, Cook and his men had time to take stock of the changes that had been wrought by the islanders' contact with the white man. They found that a Spanish ship had called at Tahiti and that influenza and venereal diseases had taken their toll of the natives. The favours of the island girls were again enjoyed by Cook's men, but nails were no longer the payment. The beautiful girls who had once innocently revelled in their own nakedness now demanded Western clothing from the sailors.

Cook's conscience was disturbed. He wrote: 'We debauch their morals and introduce among them wants and diseases which they never before knew, and which disturb the happy tranquillity which they enjoyed.'

When the *Resolution* and the *Adventurer* left Tahiti, they took with them a handsome young islander called Omai, who, on his arrival in England, was paraded like a circus monkey around London society and was even introduced to George III.

Cook remained at home with his wife and six children for less than a year before setting sail once again. With him on his final journey to Tahiti went Omai.

In August 1777 the *Resolution* dropped anchor in Matavai Bay for the last time. Omai, who was returning to his people as an ambassador of the civilised world, stepped ashore laden with fine cloth and gifts for the Tahitians. The islanders readily accepted them, then roundly snubbed Omai. Perhaps not surprisingly, the Tahitians, particularly those of noble birth, were intensely jealous of their kinsman, who had suddenly gained all the status symbols of that civilised society which they now valued so highly.

Omai had to be put by Cook on to a nearby island, Huahine, where he lived in a small house built by the crew and surrounded himself with the useless trappings of a European gentleman. Cook also had to give him firearms to protect himself from his own people.

During this visit by the English there was a new exchange of customs. Cook was introduced to a Tahitian rite which shook even this worldly-wise traveller – the human sacrifice of a prisoner, who was clubbed to death as part of a

---

Viennese authorities decided to build up a women's section in the city's police force, and recruited 60 girl constables. They gave them quarters in the city's biggest police barracks, with male police trainees in the same building but on different floors. The target of a 60-strong female force had to be scrapped, however, after it was found that 36 of the girls, all unmarried and aged between 19 and 25, were pregnant.

religious ceremony. And the Tahitians witnessed a European punishment which appalled them – a man caught stealing had his ears cut off.

Cook learned that two Spanish ships had called at the island during his absence. Their purpose had been to set up a missionary station, but they had been unable to convert the islanders and had departed after less than a year, leaving behind an abandoned makeshift church. (But the missionaries would be back – and next time their influence would be more permanent.)

Cook left the island for the last time in September 1777. He sailed for Hawaii where, at the age of 50, he was speared to death by natives.

Though Cook was an adventurer with a toughness born of the hard age in which he lived, he showed a surprising sensitivity to and understanding of the Pacific islanders. He wrote in his journal: 'It is my real opinion that it would have been far better for these poor people never to have known our superiority in the accommodations and arts that make life comfortable than, after once knowing it, to be left abandoned in their original incapacity. They can never be restored to that happy mediocrity in which they lived before we discovered them.'

The white men who followed Cook showed no such understanding of – and precious little mercy for – the 'noble savages' of Tahiti.

In 1778 Captain Bligh's *Bounty* stayed at the island for six months, during which several of the crew entered into permanent liaisons with Tahitian girls. After the *Bounty* sailed from Tahiti, the crew, led by Fletcher Christian, mutinied. Bligh was cast adrift (but survived), and the rebel *Bounty* returned to Tahiti. Some of the mutineers stayed there, others went on to the Pitcairn Isles.

In 1791 the Admiralty sent the *Pandora* to Tahiti to seek out the mutineers, who had by now been assimilated into the island life. The *Pandora*'s crew discovered that hundreds of American whaling ships had been using Tahiti as a base and that their influence on the island had been disastrous. The Tahitians were now unwashed drunkards, wearing white men's rags, their ancient customs and lifestyle forgotten.

In 1792 Bligh returned to Tahiti and reported that smallpox, dysentery and venereal disease were rife.

The final blow against this island paradise was struck in 1797 when the ship *The Duff* landed four clergymen and 34 other Britons, led by the fiercely Protestant Henry Nott. Their mission was to convert the natives to Christianity. It was a Christianity which made up in fanaticism what it lacked in mercy.

The missionaries built a church and won the islanders to it by first concentrating their influence on the chieftains. The missionaries succeeded to such an extent that within 20 years of their landing the Christian religion was obligatory in many parts of the island and 'pagans' were put to death by their own people, love outside marriage was banned, and dancing, music and even the wearing of flowers were forbidden. Guilt, the one sense the Tahitians never seemed to have known, had at last been introduced to the island.

The missionaries had brought the promise of eternal life, but nothing to lengthen the existence of the Tahitians on earth. When Captain Cook first visited Tahiti in 1769 he estimated the population at 40,000. By the turn of the century it was down to 13,000. In 1843, when the island was annexed by the French, it had dropped to less than 9,000. And the ravages of disease were to reduce yet further what had once been a proud and thriving race.

When, a century after Cook, the painter Paul Gauguin arrived on Tahiti to paint paradise, he found that he was too late. He wrote: 'Day by day, the race vanishes, decimated by the European diseases. The natives have nothing – nothing to do and nothing to think of except drinking. Many strange and picturesque things existed here once but there are no traces of them left today. Everything has gone.'

Paradise had been lost for ever.

Man-ape made monkeys out of the archaeologists

The archaeological world's greatest blunder was its long acceptance of the Piltdown Man as the missing link in man's evolution from the ape. In 1912 Charles Dawson, a lawyer and amateur geologist, collected the remains of a skull from a gravel pit near Piltdown, Sussex, and sent them to one of the world's leading experts on the history of man, Dr. Arthur Woodward of the British Museum. Together, the two men continued excavations of the pit until they had collected an amazing array of teeth, bones and prehistoric tools.

Woodward pieced together their finds – and announced that what they had unearthed was the skull of a creature, half-man, half-ape, which had lived 500,000 years ago. Although the skull was that of a woman, the find was officially named *Eoanthropus dawsoni* – Dawson's Early Man. The discovery was heralded as the first firm proof of Charles Darwin's controversial theory of evolution, and it made Dawson famous throughout the world.

Dawson continued his excavations in the Piltdown area and, over the next few years, pieced together a second skull. The finds ended upon his death in 1916, at the age of 52; others continued the search but found nothing. This was later realised not to have been so strange. For the Piltdown Man was a fake.

The skull was indeed that of a human, but the jaw and teeth were those of an orang-utan. The teeth had been filed down to look like human teeth, then the complete skull had been skilfully stained and aged before being broken up and buried in the gravel pit.

It was not until 1953 that the hoax was revealed by newly developed techniques of age-testing. And although no one has fully solved the mystery, Hoax Suspect Number One has always been Dawson. He was ambitious for academic distinction. And once, a visitor walked into his laboratory uninvited to find Dawson busy over a bubbling crucible – staining bones.

Two business ladies require a sleeping partner for beauty salon.

– London evening newspaper

Diamonds – or ostrich droppings?

Experts refused to believe the evidence of the world's richest gem-fields

The rich and famous refused to believe the evidence before their eyes when diamonds were first discovered in Hopetown, South Africa – and so chances of becoming even richer and more famous were lost.

One leading authority asserted that diamonds could not possibly exist naturally in the region. They must have been eaten elsewhere by wandering ostriches, he insisted, then dispersed throughout Hopetown in the ostriches' droppings.

He was wrong. The 'ostrich droppings' had been present for untold centuries. And they were diamonds of unsurpassed quality.

Stories had abounded of 'pretty pebbles' having been found in the area. Across an ancient map of the territory was scrawled: 'Here be diamonds'.

THE WORLD'S GREATEST MISTAKES

A couple took a taxi home after Christmas shopping in the busy West End of London in 1932. But after unloading their parcels into their house, they discovered that they had one package too many. They unwrapped it and found a leather jewel case packed with diamonds, emeralds and rubies. The honest couple took the treasure to the police who valued it at £300,000 – more than £2 million by today's values. After it had remained unclaimed for three days, the police managed to track down the owner, who still had not realised that she had mislaid the jewels. The owner was the Grand Duchess Zenia, who had escaped from Russia during the Revolution. Her treasure was part of the Russian Crown Jewels.

Yet, reminded of such stories, locals would simply smile knowingly . . . and dismiss them.

Farmer Schalk van Niekerk was less sceptical about the stories than most. Towards Christmas of 1866 he found children of Hopetown playing klip-klip, a game known elsewhere as fivestones, or jacks. They were using pebbles, and Van Niekerk quickly recognised one stone as being different from the others – excitingly different.

He stopped and picked it out of the handful of pebbles. He offered money for it to the wife of the owner of the land on which the children were playing. She laughed. Who would want to pay money for a pebble? Have it, she said. The stone, she added, had been found by one of the children in a hollow dug by a Bushman. There were lots, lots more to be found, she was sure.

Van Niekerk, astonishingly, seems to have taken no action about his discovery until the following year, when he discussed the stone with a passing trader, John O'Reilly. This itinerant, who was later to claim that he recognised the true value of the stone on sight, promised 'to find out what it really was'.

In Hopetown, O'Reilly began to boast of having found a diamond and was ragged unmercifully. Traders laughed at him and one of them bet him 'a dozen of beer' against the likelihood of such a find. A disheartened O'Reilly was prepared to throw the stone in the river. Instead, he journeyed to Colesberg, where he met further derision. Then he showed the stone to the acting civil commissioner of Colesberg, Lorenzo Boyes. At last, O'Reilly had found someone to take him seriously.

'I believe it to be a diamond,' the official declared. But others remained unconvinced. The local chemist was consulted and offered to top the wager of a dozen beers with a new hat for Boyes if the stone proved to be anything but a topaz. 'I'll take the bet,' said Boyes.

Further identification of the 'pretty pebble' could only come from an expert. Fortunately, less than 200 miles away lived the foremost geologist of the Cape Colony. He was a doctor named William Guybon Atherstone.

Boyes sent the stone to Atherstone. It was placed in an ordinary envelope, with a covering letter, and travelled on the post cart to Grahamstown, where the doctor was in practice.

The mail arrived while Atherstone sat in his garden. He opened the envelope and read the letter. He looked in the envelope, but there was no stone. He assumed it must have fallen to the ground when he opened the envelope and called his daughter to help search for it. In a wild scramble they found what appeared to be 'a dull, rounded, apparently water-worn river stone'.

Despite his experience, Atherstone had not seen an uncut diamond before, but he subjected it to several tests – and became certain that the stone which had been sent to him was a diamond. He sought confirmation from his neighbour. Father James Ricards, later the first Roman Catholic Bishop of Grahamstown. The priest tested the stone in the one way he knew would prove its identity – by cutting his initials on a pane of glass in his study (the window is now in Grahamstown Cathedral).

Atherstone wrote to Boyes: 'I congratulate you on the stone you have sent me. It is a veritable diamond, weighs 21¼ carats, and is worth £500. Where that came from there must be lots more.'

The diamond was sent to Capetown, then sent by ship to London. It was to be three months before the famous jewellers Garrards reported that it was indeed worth £500. But far from reviving enthusiasm in the Cape and South Africa as a potential source of wealth, the diamond created suspicions about its origins.

At the time, the Exposition Universelle was being held in Paris. John Blades Curry was responsible for the Cape's stand, and on hearing Garrards' findings on the diamond he tried to build up enthusiasm for this momentous discovery. He met with the same kind of ridicule and scepticism that had confronted O'Reilly. The *Illustrated London News* refused to publish a picture of it. Then Garrards refused to have anything further to do with the stone, suggesting that they had been unconsciously part of a swindle. 'If you should find diamonds in such quantities as to affect the market,' Garrards told Curry with marked sarcasm, 'we may be sorry. But with our present information we must decline to move.'

Curry then tried Sir Roderick Murchison, rated the highest geological authority in Britain, in his attempts to prove that the diamond had been found in the Cape. 'My dear sir,' Murchison replied, 'if you tell me that this diamond was picked up at the Cape of Good Hope I am bound to believe you and I do, but if you ask me to say on the strength of such an isolated fact that the Cape is a diamond-producing country I must decline. Indeed I will go further, I will stake my professional reputation on it that you have not got the matrix of the diamond in South Africa.'

Then along came O'Reilly with his second diamond, weighing nine carats. The French consul in Capetown, Ernest Heritté, reported: 'I never saw a rough diamond of greater beauty, either in respect of its crystallization or of its natural brilliancy.'

Though the rest of the world thought little of the Hopetown discoveries, the Governor of the Cape, Sir Philip Wodehouse, quickly snapped up both of O'Reilly's finds for £500 and £200 apiece.

The news again reached London. In the winter of 1868, diamond merchant Harry Emmanuel, of London's Hatton Garden, sent out mineralogist Professor James Gregory to investigate.

Gregory journeyed to the Vaal and Orange Rivers and gravely asserted that any diamonds in the district must have been carried in the gizzards of ostriches from some far-distant region. 'The whole story of the Cape diamond discoveries is false, and is simply one of many schemes for trying to promote the employment and expenditure of capital in searching for this precious substance in the colony.'

At the height of the controversy, experts pronounced on one of the diamonds that Professor Gregory had chosen to dismiss. It was a magnificent white diamond weighing $83\frac{1}{2}$ carats. It was to be known as the Star of Africa and amply denied Gregory's arguments.

Professor Gregory's findings were quickly forgotten. But not the learned expert's name. For years afterwards, a mis-statement or a lie about diamonds was laughingly dismissed as a 'Gregory' – in contempt for the professor who thought the world's largest diamond strike was just so much ostrich dung.

The driver of a road roller on the M5 was proud of the walkie-talkie set he kept in his cab.

One afternoon, in a storm, he signalled to his construction HQ: 'Mayday ... weather terrible ... am ditching for tonight.'

That night, a full-scale air-sea-rescue operation was launched in the Bristol Channel for the survivors of an air crash. All shipping was alerted, coastguards put on special watch, lifeboat crews ordered to stand by and an RAF plane put on readiness.

We've captured the Loch Ness Monster

S ightings of the famous Loch Ness Monster have been reported for more
than 1,000 years. But in 1972 experts believed they had at last captured
the 'beastie'.

What they did not know was that, some weeks earlier, the crew of a British
cargo vessel taking live elephant seals from the Falkland Islands to a zoo in
England had found one of the seals dead. They threw the body overboard. It
was picked up in the nets of a fishing boat and, for a prank, the fishermen
dumped the body in Loch Ness.

It was found there by zoologists organising a search for the monster. The
experts packed the half-ton, 15-foot giant in ice, loaded it into a van and
headed south for England to announce their news to the world.

However, locals alerted the police to the monster-snatchers' activities and
the order was flashed to all cars: 'Nessie must not leave Scotland – she belongs
to us.' Roadblocks were set up, the van was stopped on the Forth Road
Bridge, and 'Nessie' was impounded by the police.

It was only after a blaze of publicity that the true identity of the creature
was revealed.

Chapter Two

Sea and Air

When man tackles the elements, his fallibility is only too clearly displayed. It wasn't an iceberg that sank the *Titanic* – it was human error. It wasn't a storm that caused the R101 airship to crash – it was one man's pride. The following pages contain some of the greatest disasters the world has ever known, plus a few of the sillier mistakes that men have made when they have taken to the sea and the sky.

The Curse of the Pharaohs

Death awaited the discoverers of Tutankhamun's tomb

Death will come to those who disturb the sleep of the Pharaohs . . .' That was the warning found inscribed in the tomb of the Egyptian boy king Tutankhamun at Luxor when it was opened in February 1923 – for the first time in 3,000 years.

The man who led the expedition to Egypt to excavate the ancient tomb was an Englishman, 57-year-old Lord Carnarvon. And the Curse of the Pharaohs was well known to him. He knew what had happened to the man who, in the late 19th century, had brought another Pharaoh's coffin back to England. Arthur Weigall, one of the men in Lord Carnarvon's team, had told him all about the owner of that coffin: 'No sooner had he obtained the coffin than he lost his arm when his gun exploded. The ship in which the coffin was sent home was wrecked. The house in which it was kept was burnt down. The photographer who took a picture of it shot himself. A lady friend of whom the owner was very fond was lost at sea. The list of accidents and misfortunes charged to the spirit connected with the coffin is now of enormous length.'

But before the expedition went down into the tomb of Tutankhamun, Weigall heard Carnarvon make light of the Curse. Weigall warned: 'If he goes down in that spirit, I give him two months to live.'

Carnarvon's scorn of the Curse was perhaps only bravado. For two months earlier, he had received a letter from a well-known mystic of the day, Count Hamon. The cryptic message read: 'Lord Carnarvon not to enter tomb. Disobey at peril. If ignored will suffer sickness. Not recover. Death will claim him in Egypt.'

The English nobleman was so concerned about this warning that he twice consulted a fortune-teller – who twice forecast Carnarvon's early death in mysterious circumstances.

And within two months of breaking into Tutankhamun's tomb, Carnarvon *was* dead. Moreover, within six years, 12 more of those who had been present when the funerary chamber had been breached had also died prematurely. And over the years that followed, the Curse of the Pharaohs claimed several more victims among those who had been associated with the fateful expedition. One of them was the man who had twice warned Carnarvon of disaster – Weigall.

The sinister saga began in April of 1923 when one morning Carnarvon awoke in his Cairo hotel room and said: 'I feel like hell.' By the time his son arrived at the hotel, Carnarvon was unconscious. That night he died. His death was attributed to a mosquito bite – which was noted to be in the same place as a blemish on the mummified body of King Tutankhamun.

Carnarvon's son was resting in an adjoining room at the moment his father died. He said: 'The lights suddenly went out all over Cairo. We lit candles and prayed.'

Shortly afterwards there was another death at the hotel. American archaeologist Arthur Mace, who had been one of the leading members of the expedition, complained of tiredness, suddenly went into a coma and died before doctors could even diagnose what was wrong with him.

Deaths followed one upon another. A close friend of Carnarvon, George Gould, rushed to Egypt as soon as he heard of the earl's death. Gould visited the Pharaoh's tomb. The next day he had a high fever. He died within 12 hours. Radiologist Archibald Reid, who X-rayed Tutankhamun's body, complained of exhaustion. He went home to England and died shortly afterwards. Carnarvon's personal secretary on the expedition, Richard Bethell, was found dead in bed from apparent heart failure. British industrialist Joel Wool was one of the first visitors to the tomb. He died soon afterwards from a mysterious fever. By 1930, only two of the original team of excavators who had broken into the tomb were still alive.

The Curse of the Pharaohs was still taking its toll half a century later. In 1970, the sole survivor of the Tutankhamun expedition, 70-year-old Richard Adamson, gave a television interview to 'explode the myth' of the death curse.

Mourners at a funeral in Moinesti, Rumania, were astonished to see a face peering down on them from the open coffin as it was being carried shoulder-high across a road outside the cemetery.

The 'body' – a woman – then leaped out of the coffin and ran off down the road.

She ran straight into the path of a car, was knocked down and killed.

THE WORLD'S GREATEST MISTAKES

He told viewers: 'I don't believe in the myth for one moment.' Afterwards, as he left the Norwich television studios, his taxi collided with a tractor, throwing him out on to the road. A passing lorry missed his head by inches.

It was the third time that Adamson, who had been security guard to Lord Carnarvon's expedition, had tried to put paid to the legend. The first time he spoke against it, his wife died within 48 hours. The second time, his son broke his back in a plane crash. After the third occasion, Adamson, recovering in hospital from head injuries, said: 'Until now, I refused to believe that there was any connection between the Curse and what happened to my family. But now I am having second thoughts.'

A year later, the Curse of the Pharaohs struck again, but this time Tutankhamun had no hand in it. British Egyptologist Professor Walter Emery was digging for the tomb of the god of medicine, Imhotep, at Sakkara, near the Pyramids, when he uncovered a statue of Osiris, the god of death. The professor was handling the statue when he fell dead from a cerebral thrombosis.

Fears of the Curse of the Pharaohs were revived in 1972 when the golden mask of Tutankhamun was crated for shipment to Britain for an exhibition at London's British Museum to mark the 50th anniversary of the tomb's discovery.

In charge of the operation was Dr. Gamal Mehrez, director-general of the antiquities department of the Cairo Museum, where he was responsible for the safe keeping of 20 ancient mummies. Dr. Mehrez did not believe in the Curse – not even after his predecessor had suddenly died within hours of signing an agreement to send the treasures of Tutankhamun to Paris. Mehrez said: 'I, more than anyone else in the world, have been involved with the tombs and mummies of the Pharaohs. Yet I am still alive. I'm the living proof that all the tragedies associated with the Pharaohs are just coincidence. I don't believe in the Curse for one moment.'

On February 3, 1972, the shippers arrived at the Cairo Museum to remove the crated golden mask of Tutankhamun and prepare it for its journey to London. That day, Dr. Mehrez died. He was 52. The cause of his death was given as circulatory collapse.

Unperturbed, the organisers of the exhibition continued with the arrangements. A Royal Air Force Transport Command aircraft was loaned for the job of transporting the priceless relics to Britain. But within five years of the flight, six members of the plane's crew were to be struck by death or ill fortune.

During the flight, Chief Technical Officer Ian Lansdowne jokingly kicked a box containing Tutankhamun's death mask. He said: 'I've just kicked the most expensive thing in the world.' That leg was later in plaster for five months, badly broken after a ladder inexplicably collapsed under Lansdowne.

The aircraft's navigator, Lieutenant Jim Webb, lost all his possessions after

Above The mummy of Tutankhamun.

Above right Lord Carnarvon (left)
entering the tomb of Tutankhamun.

Right The Earl of Carnarvon.

his home was destroyed by fire. A girl aboard the plane quit the RAF after a head operation left her bald.

A steward, Sergeant Brian Rounsfall, said: 'On the flight back, we played cards on the coffin case. Then we all took it in turns to sit on the case containing the death mask and we laughed and joked about it. We were not being disrespectful – it was just a bit of fun.' Sergeant Rounsfall was 35 at the time. In the following four years, he suffered two heart attacks, but survived, a worried man.

Less lucky were Lieutenant Rick Laurie, chief pilot aboard the Britannia aircraft, and Engineer Ken Parkinson. Both were perfectly fit men; both died of heart attacks.

Parkinson's wife said: 'My husband suffered a heart attack every year at about the same time as the flight.' The last attack, in 1978, killed him. He was 45.

Chief pilot Laurie died two years before him. At the time, his wife said: 'It's the Curse of Tutankhamun – the Curse has killed him.' He was just 40.

Is there any logical explanation for the mysterious deaths of so many people? Journalist Phillip Vandenberg studied the legend of the Curse of the Pharaohs for years. He came up with a fascinating suggestion. In his book, *The Curse of the Pharaohs*, he says that the tombs within the Pyramids were perfect breeding grounds for bacteria which could develop new and unknown strains over the centuries and could maintain their potency until the present day.

He also points out that the ancient Egyptians were experts in poison. Some poisons do not have to be swallowed to kill – they can prove lethal by penetrating the skin. Poisonous substances were used in wall paintings within the tombs, which were then sealed and made airtight. Grave-robbers who in ancient days raided the tombs always first bored a small hole through the chamber wall to allow fresh air to circulate before they broke in to plunder the Pharaohs' riches.

But the most extraordinary explanation of all for the Curse was put forward in 1949. It came from the atomic scientist Professor Louis Bulgarini. He said: 'It is definitely possible that the ancient Egyptians used atomic radiation to protect their holy places. The floors of the tombs could have been covered with uranium. Or the graves could have been finished with radio-active rock.

Mr. Sid Rawle, aged 29, a former gravedigger, is now the editor of an underground newspaper.

– Manchester newspaper

Rock containing both gold and uranium was mined in Egypt 3,000 years ago. Such radiation could kill a man today.'

If there is any truth in the belief that the ancient Pharaohs can be held responsible for 20th-century deaths, then there is one case which overshadows all others. In 1912, a liner was crossing the Atlantic with a valuable cargo – an Egyptian mummy. It was the body of a prophetess who lived during the reign of Tutankhamun's father-in-law, Akhenaton. An ornament found with the mummy bore a spell: 'Awake from the dream in which you sleep and you will triumph over all that is done against you.' Because of its value, the mummy was not carried in the liner's hold, but in a compartment behind the bridge on which stood the captain, whose errors of judgment played a part in causing his ship to sink. The story of the sinking of that ship, and of the death of 1,513 passengers aboard her, is told elsewhere in this book. Her name was the *Titanic*.

The 'Unsinkable' Titanic

The first SOS signal in history failed to save 1,513 men, women and children

The sea was as smooth as a millpond and the sky brilliant with stars when Frederick Fleet, the look-out in the crow's nest, spotted the towering grey mountain of ice.

'Iceberg right ahead,' he shouted down his telephone to the bridge. And so began two hours and 40 minutes of incredulity, fear, and finally horror for the 2,300 passengers of the White Star liner – the 'unsinkable' *Titanic*. For that was all the time that it took, from the moment the iceberg was sighted, for the biggest and supposedly safest liner in the world to sink beneath the icy waters of the North Atlantic.

It was 11.40 p.m. on April 14, 1912, when the warning call came from the crow's nest. Immediately, the huge vessel swung to port – but not soon enough. The *Titanic* scraped along the jagged side of the iceberg.

On the bridge, officers congratulated themselves on a near-miss. But below the water line, the Atlantic Ocean poured in through a 300-foot gash in the ship's plates.

George Rowe was one of the quartermasters on the *Titanic*. This is how he described the crash: 'The first I knew of the disaster was when I felt a peculiar shiver run through the vessel. It became icy cold and my breath froze in the air. Then I saw the iceberg – and I shall never forget it.

'At first I thought we had hit a windjammer as I caught a glimpse of something sliding past the ship on the starboard side. In the glare from the light of thousands of portholes, the smooth surface looked just like wet canvas.

'I ran over to the side and realised that I was looking at an iceberg. It was so big that it seemed to fill the sky. It was a giant among icebergs and towered menacingly even above the bridge.

'For a few seconds I gazed at it unbelievingly. It was just a few feet away and I felt I could have touched it. Then it was gone – swallowed up in the blackness.'

Even when the ship's master, Captain Ernest Smith, Commodore of the White Star fleet, realised that the hull of the world's wondership had been breached, he showed no signs of alarm. After all, the *Titanic* was 'unsinkable'. That had been the proud boast when the liner had left Southampton for New York four days earlier, at the start of her maiden voyage.

The ship's 850-foot-long hull had been made up of 14 watertight compartments. And the ship had a double bottom. It was the safest in the world. In fact, the *Titanic* could have remained afloat with all of her first four watertight compartments flooded. But the iceberg had torn through the first five – and, because of some strange quirk in the ship's design, Bulkhead Number Five did not stretch up as high into the ship as the others. With the first four compartments flooded, the liner's bows would dip, the water would flow over Bulkhead Number Five into the sixth compartment . . . then into the seventh

---

The Meteorological Office at Bracknell, Berkshire, was asked by a governmental committee for the official ruling on when winter begins and when it ends. The committee expected an answer that would pin down the times to precise seconds. The answer given, however, was: 'Winter begins when all the leaves have fallen off the trees and ends when the bulbs start coming up again.'

The *Titanic*'s distress call.

... and the eighth. ... And it would then simply be a matter of time. ...

The myth of the *Titanic*'s unsinkability was only one of an incredible combination of human errors, without which neither the liner nor the 1,513 lives need have been lost.

Why was the *Titanic* travelling so fast – 22 knots – when a mass of icebergs had been reported in the area? Just before the crash, the liner was at 'full ahead', despite the fact that during that evening wireless signals had been received from other vessels including the *Baltic*, containing the information that she was heading straight into an icefield.

The *Baltic*'s message had been handed to George Ismay, the line's managing director, who showed it to some of the passengers before it was posted in the chart room at 7.15 p.m.

Why was the *Titanic*'s radio out of contact with other shipping? A final ice-warning message was sent to the liner by the *Messaba* at 9.40 p.m. It is known that the message was received by the *Titanic*. But it was never acknowledged, and it is doubtful whether it ever reached the bridge.

If that message had got through and been heeded by Captain Smith, 1,513 lives would certainly have been saved. For, less than an hour earlier, Smith had been heard discussing the danger of icebergs with his officer of the watch. Smith gave orders for a strict look-out to be kept, but he did not feel that the situation was serious enough to warrant a cut in speed.

Why, also, did the *Titanic* have only 16 lifeboats – with just 1,250 seats for the 2,300 people on board? The liner had sufficient fittings to handle 48 lifeboats.

The White Star Line was perfectly within its legal rights to provide such an inadequate number of boats. British Board of Trade regulations covering the ship had been drawn up in 1894 and were now ridiculously out of date. The rules specified the number of lifeboats to be carried by passenger ships of more than 10,000 tons. Liners had grown in size dramatically since then – the *Titanic* was 46,328 tons – yet the regulations had never been amended.

But the biggest question mark of all hangs over the role of another passenger ship – the *Californian*, one of the vessels that had earlier sent ice warnings to the *Titanic*. Because of the ice danger, it had stopped only about eight miles away from the spot where the *Titanic* was slowly sinking. Yet it did not arrive on the scene until after the *Titanic* had slipped beneath the surface of the Atlantic.

Aboard the 6,000-ton *Californian* it had been an uneventful night. Earlier in the evening, the wireless operator had tried to break in on messages being sent out by the *Titanic* in order to warn of the ice danger. No one knows the exact nature of the warning that he eventually sent. What is known is that he felt snubbed by its ungracious reception. At the end of his duty, he went down to his bunk after switching off his wireless set. The time was 11.30 – just ten minutes before the *Titanic* hit the iceberg.

On the bridge of the *Californian*, the third officer watched the lights of the *Titanic* speeding towards them. He reported to the ship's master, Captain Stanley Lord, who suggested that they try to contact the liner by morse light. They tried over and over again. But there was no response whatever from the *Titanic*, which sped by into the icefield.

Aboard the *Titanic*, the passengers were at first puzzled rather than frightened by the slight listing of the ship. As they walked up the stairways on to the deck to find out what had happened, there was no sign of panic. They firmly believed the boasts about the liner's invincibility.

Although the *Titanic* struck the iceberg at 11.40 p.m., it was not until five minutes after midnight that the order was given: 'Uncover the lifeboats.' As crewmen pulled off the boats' canvas covers, the ship's band struck up a rag-time tune – and kept on playing.

Later there was a bang and a flash as the first distress rocket went off. The passengers at last began to realise that they were in danger. Until then, people had been reluctant to get into the lifeboats. Wives had pleaded with crewmen to be allowed to stay with their husbands. Husbands had urged them to get into the boats. Now, officers called out: 'Women and children first,' and no one argued.

One of the first-class passengers, Lady Duff Gordon, had refused to get into several boats. Then she and her husband found themselves standing beside

77

one of the officers who was in charge of a small lifeboat and who had been having little success in persuading passengers to get into it. The officer said: 'Do get into the boat, madam. I shall be so pleased if you would.' Lady Duff Gordon stepped into the lifeboat.

American millionaire Benjamin Guggenheim had been wrapped in warm clothing by his steward. He appeared on deck, sought out his valet and re-appeared later wearing full evening dress, 'so that I will go down like a gentleman.'

Others who were to go down with the ship that night were its captain; its designer, Thomas Andrews; millionaire Isadore Strauss; Colonel John Jacob Astor, who was returning from honeymoon with his bride; and famed journalist William Stead.

Stead would never have died if he had heeded his own warning. For in 1892 he had written a short story describing his vision of a mighty liner sinking in northern waters with the loss of hundreds of lives. Stead, who was a spiritualist, had foreseen his own death.

Death indeed was now not far away for most of the passengers of the *Titanic*. In the wireless room, operator John Phillips tapped out 'CQD' ... 'CQD' ... over and over again. CQD was the traditional maritime distress call of the period. But an international convention had just decided to recommend the use of the signal SOS instead. So halfway through the night, Phillips decided to change signals – and sent out the first SOS in history.

Half a dozen ships began racing to the scene. But the two ships closest to the *Titanic* did not hear the desperate calls for help. Aboard the stationary *Californian*, the wireless operator was fast asleep. And 60 miles away the Cunard liner *Carpathia* was steaming southwards with its wireless operator away from his set, on the ship's bridge. When he did return to the wireless room, the time was almost half past midnight. He decided to put through a courtesy call to the great new liner he knew to be in the vicinity. Unbelievingly, he heard the reply: 'SOS. We have struck an iceberg. Come at once.'

At two o'clock the *Titanic*'s wireless operator received the order: 'Abandon ship. It's every man for himself.' He ignored it and continued tapping out 'SOS ... SOS' until the very last moment.

British publishers Ladybird Books were surprised to receive an order from the Ministry of Defence for a set of books for its staff explaining how computers work. The firm wrote back pointing out that the books were designed for children aged nine and upwards. The Defence Ministry replied confirming the order.

In one of the last overcrowded lifeboats to leave the *Titanic* stood Mrs. Emily Richards, then 24, and off to join her husband in the USA. She had her 10-month-old baby, George, in her arms. She said later: 'We pulled away from the liner. The sea was full of wreckage and bodies. Some people had jumped overboard and were screaming for help. The sea was very icy. We wanted to pick them up but our boat was overloaded already.'

As the lifeboats drifted away from the doomed liner, the passengers who had escaped looked back helplessly on a scene that they thought could only have been dreamed up in hell.

The *Titanic* lay with rows and rows of lights still blazing on a millpond sea dotted with icebergs. The ship was still not far from the monstrous grey mass of the giant iceberg that it had struck.

The liner's four funnels, towering 175 feet above its keel, stood out against the starry sky. They leaned forward at a crazy angle. And at 2.20 a.m. the *Titanic* began to slip beneath the surface. The band was still playing, its music carrying eerily across the still expanse of sea. But now the ragtime had ended, and a hymn was struck up. Some survivors remember it as the old hymn *Autumn*; others say it was *Nearer My God To Thee*. The ship's lights illuminated hundreds of spider-like figures clinging to the decks and to the sides of the liner as its propellers were lifted above the water line. One by one, they fell or jumped into the sea to certain, freezing death.

'There was a long, rumbling boom, like distant thunder,' said Emily Richards. 'The lights went out, flashed on again, then went out for good. The stern rose until it was pointing almost straight up in the air. Then the *Titanic* slipped swiftly and smoothly out of sight.'

The lifeboats packed with shivering survivors drifted until dawn, when the liner *Carpathia* arrived on the scene and picked up 705 of them.

Most of the survivors were first- and second-class ticket holders. These had been given priority in the lifeboats, and all their children were saved. Of the steerage children only a third survived.

The officers on the bridge of the *Californian* had kept occasional watch on the *Titanic* through binoculars. They had noted how, like their own ship, it had stopped amid the ice. They had watched the flickering lights in the distance. They had again tried to contact the *Titanic* by morse light, but had received no response and given up. Then, at 12.45 a.m., they had seen rockets bursting into the air over the *Titanic*. They had thought that such a display of fireworks was most curious, but did not investigate. At 2.20 a.m. the men on the *Californian* noticed that the lights in the distance had disappeared. They took no action.

Courts of inquiry in Britain and America later severely censured Captain Lord of the *Californian* for failing to appreciate the nature of the rocket signals reported to him. Lord contested the findings right up to his death in 1962.

The inquiries also found that Captain Smith had made a mistake in not turning south or reducing speed. But no blame was attached to his course of action, because it was common practice at the time.

The British inquiry also made some important recommendations. It advised that the number of lifeboats on a ship should be based on the number of people carried and not on tonnage, that ship's wirelesses should be manned night and day, and it warned that any captain running his ship full speed into an icefield in future would lay himself open to the charge of negligence.

All of which came too late to save those who perished.

It was a disaster that, strangely, had been foreshadowed not only by William Stead's short story but, in uncanny detail, in a novel published 14 years earlier.

The book, written by Morgan Robertson, told the story of the biggest and most luxurious liner ever built . . . of how it set out from Southampton to New York on its maiden voyage . . . of how it hit an iceberg in the North Atlantic . . . of how its hull was torn open beneath the waterline . . . and of how it sank with an appalling loss of life because it failed to carry enough lifeboats.

The name of the ship was the *Titan*.

Terror of the aircraft stowaways

No one saw their dash to the plane. The two young men who had been hiding behind a ramp at Havana Airport sprinted across the blazing hot runway until they were in the shade of one of the giant wings of a DC8 airliner. The aircraft was halted at the end of the main runway, waiting for clearance for take-off. The two men clambered on to the wheels and climbed up the landing gear. Then they huddled in the wheel bay – the space inside the wing which houses the undercarriage in flight.

Within minutes Armando Ramirez and George Blanco were airborne. The DC8 of Iberian Airways thundered down the runway and soared into the blue Caribbean sky to start its transatlantic journey to Madrid. The undercarriage was retracted and the two men squeezed themselves against the sides of the wheel bay so that they would not be squashed by the landing gear. The wheel bay door closed beneath them and all was darkness, roaring engines and whistling wind.

Ramirez and Blanco relaxed for the first time since putting into action their daring plan to escape from Fidel Castro's communist regime in Cuba. They had fled their homeland with no possessions whatsoever – nothing that could possibly have slowed that vital dash across the runway at Havana. They were also dressed lightly, in thin trousers and short-sleeved shirts.

As the airport fell away behind the DC8, Ramirez huddled tighter in his corner. He realised now that this was going to be a long, cold journey. Blanco edged himself around the retracted undercarriage seeking a more comfortable position in which to spend his first flight. He ended up crouched over the wheels.

At that moment a warning light flashed on the flight deck instrument panel. Something was wrong with the undercarriage. It had not locked home. The first officer flicked a switch and the landing gear began descending again. Blanco was taken by surprise as the wheels jolted downwards. With a scream that was muffled by the slipstream, he lost his grip and fell out of the wheel bay to his death.

The undercarriage retracted once more, and this time no red light flashed on the controls. The pilot was satisfied. For Ramirez, however, the journey was becoming a nightmare. He had been able to do nothing to save his friend, and now that the plane was heading for its cruising altitude of 30,000 feet the cold in the wheel bay was becoming intolerable. It was increasingly difficult to breathe, too. Ramirez passed out.

During the Spanish airliner's 4,500-mile flight, the temperature in the wheel bay fell to $-40°$ Centigrade and the rarefied atmosphere became almost devoid of oxygen. But the young Cuban was tough. As the DC8 landed at Madrid he regained consciousness briefly, and astonished ground staff watched him fall out of the wheel bay on to the tarmac.

Ramirez recovered in hospital to begin his self-imposed exile.

Space scientist Dr. Hubert Strughold wanted to disprove the old and unscientific adage: 'A pilot flies by the seat of his pants.'

He injected his buttocks with the anaesthetic novocaine until his posterior was completely numb. Then Dr. Strughold, who in the 1960s was head of America's Space Medicine Programme, took off as passenger in a jet plane.

The pilot looped, rolled and went through every acrobatic trick in the book. Dr. Strughold, who had flown without upset many times before, returned to earth feeling very ill. He announced: 'The pants are one of the pilot's most valuable flight instruments.'

Hang on, we're about to land!

It was a long and boring flight for 20-year-old Harry Griffiths, from Toronto. It was December, 1942, and the Boston bomber of which he was co-pilot was being ferried from one airfield to another. It was now droning along at 7,000 feet over Lake St. Louis, Quebec. The only people aboard were Griffiths and the American pilot.

At this stage of the flight, Griffiths was due to check the bomb-bay. He scrambled into the cramped compartment, but, failing to notice that the bomb-bay doors had not fully closed, he dropped out of the plane. As he did so, he grabbed the edge of one of the bomb doors and hung on for his life, screaming for help.

The pilot, 29-year-old Sid Gerow, from Minnesota, heard him but could not leave the controls to haul him aboard. Instead, he brought his plane down until it was skimming the ice of frozen Lake St. Louis at 100 miles an hour – as low a speed as he dared fly for fear of stalling. Griffiths then let go his hold, dropped 20 feet and skidded over ice and through snow for 1,000 yards.

The bomber's pilot flew off, radioing for a rescue team. But it was a local farmer who found the young flyer. Griffiths was sitting in the snow, cold and shaken but smiling. He had suffered only cuts and bruises.

Equally lucky was the steward aboard an Eastern Airlines Dakota who was sucked out of the plane when the cabin door flew open at 2,500 feet above Tulsa, Oklahoma, in 1949. As he was swept into the slipstream, his left foot became wedged between the door and one of the hinges.

The pilot made an emergency landing at Tulsa. Ambulancemen, ground staff and passengers rushed to see if anything was left of the steward. They found him lying on the tarmac, unconscious but unhurt. He had fainted as soon as the plane landed.

A dealer in Connecticut advertised a car for '1,395 bananas' – meaning $1,395.

A woman turned up and offered him 25 bananas deposit and, when he refused to accept them, sued the dealer for false advertising.

She won her case, produced the other 1,370 bananas and drove off in the car.

The R101 inferno

One man's pride destroyed the airship dream

It was the most unnecessary fiasco in the history of flying. The tragedy of the R101 airship is not just the story of a disaster which claimed 48 lives. It is an unbelievable catalogue of inefficiency, incompetence, pride, prestige and petty politics.

It all began when the Vickers aircraft and engineering firm, the most experienced builders of airships in Britain, proposed to the Conservative government of 1923 that giant airships be used for passenger services to different parts of the Empire. The government would commission them – and Vickers would, of course, build them.

Before a decision could be made, the Conservatives fell, and in 1924 the first Labour Parliament came to power on promises of nationalisation and State control. A new success for robustly capitalist Vickers did not fit into their scheme of things. So Ramsay MacDonald's men made the most astonishing decision. They decided to commission not one, but two airships to exactly the same specification. The R100, a capitalist airship, and the R101, a socialist airship. One to be made by Vickers and one by the Air Ministry. The government would then decide which of the two was the better craft.

THE WORLD'S GREATEST MISTAKES

The capitalist team's chief calculator was a man called Nevil Shute Norway – now better known as novelist Nevil Shute. Many years after the disaster, he wrote: 'The controversy between capitalism and State enterprise had been argued, tested and fought in many ways, but the airship venture in Britain was the most curious of them all.'

Through the mid-1920s the two ships were designed and slowly took shape. The R100 was built in a leaky World War One airship hangar at Howden, Yorkshire. Local labour was recruited for much of the manual work – and that presented the capitalist team with their most unexpected problem. According to Shute, the local women were 'filthy in appearance and habits, and incredibly foul-mouthed. Promiscuous intercourse was going on merrily in every dark corner.'

Lord Thomson of Cardington, Labour's air minister, was responsible for the R101, and it was at Cardington, near Bedford, that the airship was built. The problems there were technical. And when they appeared they tended to be swept under the carpet.

Extraordinarily, the Air Ministry decided that petrol engines would be unsafe for their airship and chose diesel engines instead. The Cardington design team argued against the decision but were ignored. So eight-cylinder diesel units were ordered – engines originally designed for railway locomotives. They weighed twice as much as the R100's petrol-power units, vibrated alarmingly and were far less efficient.

Indeed, so little check was kept on the weight of all the gadgetry that was being built into the R101 that it was not until the airship was first inflated and tested that it was discovered that its lifting power was about half of that which it should have been. The team immediately began taking out of the craft all the extra equipment which they had confidently built into it.

The effect was disastrous. The airship was unbalanced. The bags of hydrogen rolled around inside the craft. It bucked alarmingly in flight. The outer casing split time and time again and had to be covered with patches. The fins were beautifully streamlined but tended to stall. The gas valves were so sensitive that they leaked perpetually. The propellers broke when put into reverse, and a heavy backward-facing engine had to be fitted in order that the airship could manoeuvre when docking.

Many such problems were also encountered – and surmounted – by the Vickers team, led by designer Barnes Wallis, who was to become famous in World War Two for his dam-busting bouncing bomb. But such was the rivalry between Wallis and R101 chief designer Lieutenant-Colonel Victor Richmond that, throughout the five years of construction, neither man visited or even wrote to the other to discuss common problems.

The R101 was finished first. A large VIP crowd was invited to Cardington

R101 airship moored to its mast, seen from the surrounding countryside.

The unveiling of the R101 memorial at Allone, near Beauvais.

to marvel at the enormous airship's graceful lines as it swung gently on its mooring tower. Two hundred yards long and filled with 5 million cubic feet of hydrogen, it was the largest airship in the world.

The R100 lacked the beauty of its sister ship, but had one rather important advantage over it. It could fly safely. In growing desperation, the Cardington team cut their airship in two, stuffed an extra gas tank in the middle, put the craft together again and once more hauled it to its mooring tower. Within minutes, the whole skin of the airship began rippling in the wind, and a 90-foot gash opened up along its side.

The public were never told of these snags, and on June 28, 1930, the R101, a victim of its own over-inflated publicity, was flown to Hendon to take part in an air display. The crowds gasped as the airship suddenly dipped its nose and dived spectacularly before pulling up sharply. They were in even greater awe when the craft, already too low for comfort, repeated the manoeuvre and pulled out of its dive just 500 feet above the 100,000-strong crowd.

What the spectators did not know was that the spectacle was unplanned – and that the sweating coxswain had been struggling at the controls to avert disaster.

Neither were they told that when the R101 was examined afterwards, more than 60 holes were found in the hydrogen bags. The highly inflammable gas was pouring out everywhere.

A brave Air Ministry inspector reported: 'Until this matter is seriously taken in hand and remedied I cannot recommend the extension of the present permit-to-fly or the issue of any further permit or certificate.'

His report was ignored by his superiors.

Now the Cardington team were frantic. They saw the whole enterprise as a battle between capitalism and socialism, a battle that the socialists were losing. And the big test was approaching – the R100 was to fly to Canada and back, the R101 to India and back. The Cardington team suggested a postponement of both trips. The Howden team, revelling in their rivals' problems, refused to call off the R100's journey.

On July 29, 1930, seven years after Vickers first proposed the giant airship project, the R100 set off for Canada. It completed the round-trip successfully and without fuss.

As the date of the R101's planned trip to India approached, the Cardington

---

Cordon Bleu cook required for directors' dining room.
Good salary plus luncheon vouchers.

– Times

team became more alarmed. There was dissension among the designers. The Air Ministry was recommended to delay the great publicity stunt.

It was then that folly and ambition were compounded into disaster by Air Minister Lord Thomson. During the construction and testing of the R101, he had been persistently pushing behind the scenes to promote the project. Thomson, an army general before he turned socialist, was a charming man, a 55-year-old bachelor, sophisticated and much sought after by women; but he was also proud, ambitious and unswervingly stubborn.

He wanted the R101 to fly him to India without any further delays. He wanted to make a magnificent impression when the airship arrived at Karachi. His ambition was to become Viceroy of India and he hoped that the spectacle would help him achieve that aim.

Nevil Shute wrote: 'To us, watching helplessly on the sidelines, the decision to fly the R101 to India that autumn of 1930 appeared to be sheer midsummer madness.' He said of Thomson: 'He was the man primarily responsible for the organisation which produced the disaster. Under his control, practically every principle of safety in the air was abandoned.'

A final conference about the trip was held at the Air Ministry on October 2. Thomson said he wanted to start for India the next day. His staff protested. Thomson insisted. Eventually, take-off was agreed for the evening of October 4.

Thomson told the conference: 'You must not allow my natural impatience or anxiety to influence you in any way.' But no one believed that the caution was sincere. After all, he had already issued an official directive to everyone concerned in the project: 'I must insist on the programme for the Indian flight being adhered to, as I have made my plans accordingly.' He had also announced: 'The R101 is as safe as a house – at least, to the millionth chance.'

Test flying was far from complete by October 4. The R101 had not been issued with an airworthiness certificate, so the Air Ministry wrote one out for themselves. Poor-weather tests had not even been embarked on. The airship had not flown at full power.

Major G. H. Scott, who had successfully captained the R100 across the Atlantic to Canada and back, was to be the senior crew member of the R101. He had heard most of the warnings about the R101. He knew it was under-powered and unstable. But he decided to go along 'for the ride'.

Another VIP passenger was to be Air Vice-Marshal Sir Sefton Brancker, the tall, monocled director of civil aviation. He was extremely sceptical – and said so. He had seen reports on the R101's trials. He had learned that when the airship dived at Hendon it had virtually broken its back. He knew that hydrogen constantly poured from holes caused by the gas bags chafing against each other and the superstructure.

Thomson told him: 'If you are afraid to go, then don't.' Sir Sefton went.

At 6.30 on the evening of October 4, Thomson and his valet stepped aboard the R101. There were four other passengers, plus 48 crew. It was a wet, miserable evening. The leaky airship was already grossly overweight and had to drop four tons of water-ballast to get away.

At 8 p.m., while the airship was over London, it received a new weather forecast by radio. It predicted a 40 m.p.h. headwind over northern France, with low cloud and driving rain. Major Scott had the perfect excuse for listening to his own fears and turning back. After all, the R101 had never flown in any but good weather conditions. Scott discussed the report with Thomson. The airship continued on its journey. . . .

At 2 p.m., the R101 was over Beauvais, in northern France. It had travelled only 200 miles in more than seven hours and was flying dangerously low, as well as rolling and pitching a great deal. But in the control room, slung under the hull, the watch changed normally.

Inside the vast hull itself, other crewmen and passengers slept. The cabins were twin-berthed and formed the upper deck of a two-floor module sealed off from the roar of the engines and the beating of the weather. On the lower deck was the vast lounge – 60 feet long and more than 30 feet wide, with wicker settees, chairs and tables, and potted plants disguising the supporting pillars. Outside the lounge ran promenade decks with huge observation windows. Also on the lower deck were the ornate dining room, a smoking room, kitchens, and stairs leading down to the control room.

At about five minutes past two, the nose of the R101 dipped. Foreman engineer Henry Leech, alone in the smoking room, slid off the settee. His glass and soda syphon clattered from the table.

Radio operator Arthur Disley was roused from sleep. He had only just turned in after tapping out a message back to Britain. It had said: 'After an excellent supper, our distinguished passengers smoked a final cigar and have now gone to rest after the excitement of their leave-taking.' Now, Disley realised, something was wrong.

In the control car, the navigator saw that, although the altimeter recorded 1,000 feet above sea level, the airship was ominously close to the ground. He had not realised that the seemingly slight hills around Beauvais were so high.

THE WORLD'S GREATEST MISTAKES

Engineers John Binks and Albert Bell were chatting in one of the gangways. Both fell with a bump when the ship dived.

Rigger Alf Church was walking to the crew area at the end of his term of duty when he heard an officer shout: 'Release emergency ballast.' Church ran back to his post and jettisoned half a ton of water from the nose.

The R101 righted itself and again roared forward against the wind and rain. In the smoking room, Leech picked up the glasses and the soda syphon. They were unbroken. He replaced them on the table and lounged back again on the settee.

In Beauvais, the town clock had not long struck two, and several citizens were leaning out of their windows watching the strange airship sail by. It passed over the centre of the town, about 200 yards above the ground. It was rolling and dipping as it vanished beyond a wood.

On the edge of the wood, 56-year-old Alfred Roubaille was out poaching, hoping to bag a couple of rabbits for his family's Sunday lunch. He plodded across the sodden ground, stopping every now and then to lay his snares.

Roubaille heard a roaring of engines above. He looked up – and fled to the shelter of the trees. From there, he – and he alone – saw from start to finish a catastrophe which shook the world.

The R101 was flying straight and level, but very low. Suddenly the nose of the airship dipped for the second time. The airship's telegraph rang. Coxswain Oughton wrestled with the controls. The elevators did not respond. The nose of the ship, somewhere forward of the huge lettering R101, had been bared. The frail fabric had split. The wind was gusting in and the hydrogen was pouring out.

Alfred Roubaille said later: 'The airship started to sink towards the ground. She was moving slowly forward and pointing her nose downwards.'

The first officer, Lieutenant-Commander Atherstone, peered at the looming earth through the window of the control room. He realised the airship was doomed. He ordered Chief Coxswain Hunt to race through the hull and alert everyone that the ship was about to crash.

Radio operator Disley heard Hunt scream: 'We're down, lads.' Disley swung his legs from his bunk. Leech leapt from the smoking room settee. In the engine-gondolas suspended beneath the hull, engineers Cook, Bell, Binks and Savory watched horrified as the ground came up to meet them.

Roubaille said: 'Just as the airship was nearing the ground, a strong gust of wind blew her down hard.'

The R101 pancaked into the moist earth of a flat field no more than a hundred yards from the poacher. For a moment, the only sound was the gush of escaping gas. Then came the explosions.

A blinding flash lit the sky. Two further explosions quickly followed, and an unbelievable white inferno engulfed the once-majestic airship.

Engineer Victor Savory was blinded by the flash of flame that seared in through the open door of his gondola. He leapt for the opening, landed on the soft soil and fled.

His colleague, Albert Cook, tried to get out of his gondola door but found it blocked by a girder, dripping with blazing cellulose from the hull.

'I lay down and gave up,' he said. 'But only for a moment.'

Then Cook dragged away the girder with his bare hands and, pitifully burned, hurled himself into some undergrowth.

Engineers Binks and Bell believed they were lost when their gondola became engulfed in flame. Then came the miracle . . . a ballast tank of water above the gondola burst. The water cascaded on to the gondola and put out the flames. They fled.

Leech was still in the smoking room. He had just got up from the settee when the blazing metal ceiling crashed down on it. He flattened himself on to the floor, then crawled on all fours towards a hole that had opened in the wall. He leapt through the flaming envelope of the airship.

Leech was out, safe. But then he heard the cries of Disley, who was inside the blazing hull, clawing at it and even trying to bite an opening in it with his teeth. Leech ran back into the inferno to help him, but suddenly a fiery hole opened up in the hull and Disley flung himself through it. Leech and Disley raced away across the field together.

Savory, Cook, Binks, Bell, Leech and Disley. Of the 54 people aboard the R101, they were the only survivors.

Poacher Roubaille said: 'I heard people in the wreckage crying for help. I was a hundred yards away and the heat was awful. I ran as hard as I could away from that place.'

For the dying victims of a ship that had been built by stubborn pride, for the man who had been the most stubborn and proud of them all, there was no hope on earth of escape from the hungry flames.

Irish railway officials made a mistake when they wrote an offhand reply to fiery playwright Brendan Behan in a dispute over a fare refund. They signed their letter 'for N. H. Briant'. Behan wrote back: 'Dear for N. H. Briant, If you don't want to give me back my 12 quid, say so. I've more to do than to be answering your silly letters. I'm usually paid more than 12 quid for writing as much as this. For Brendan Behan, Brendan Behan.'

Saga of the 'battleship-submarines'

During World War One, Britain decided to build a new type of giant submarine – a sort of underwater battleship that would give the Allies command below the waves as well as above them. The new submarines were labelled K-boats.

The first two flotillas of K-boats were ready for action by the end of 1917. But when they were put to the test, these 325-foot steam-powered monsters of the deep proved to be unmanoeuvrable on the surface, slow and clumsy when diving and, once underwater, very difficult to bring to the surface again. This was their lamentable track record:

Fire broke out aboard the K-2 on its first test dive. K-3 inexplicably dived to the sea bed on its first test – with the Prince of Wales, later to become George VI, aboard. The boat eventually resurfaced and its illustrious passenger was saved.

Later, on exercise, K-3 was rammed and sunk by K-6. K-4 ran aground. K-5 sank and its crew died. K-6 got stuck on the sea bed. K-7 ran down K-17 on exercise, putting itself out of action for good.

K-14 sprang a leak before it had even got out of port on its first trials. And later, on exercises in the North Sea, it was run down and sunk by K-22. K-17, on the same exercise, went out of control and sank after colliding with both an escorting cruiser and with K-7. Finally, K-22 was damaged beyond repair after getting in the way of yet another cruiser.

The K-boats operation was scrapped in 1918 after it had claimed 250 British lives but not one German sailor was killed.

A business man, fed up with the foul smell from a sausage skin factory near his home in Welwyn Garden City, Hertfordshire, bought the entire plant.

He was then told by the local authority that the factory's use must still be confined to trades within the category of 'existing rights'.

Apart from sausage skin manufacture, these included the boiling of blood, the breeding of maggots and the preparation of glue and manure.

The Torrey Canyon disaster

Captain is blamed for the world's worst oil pollution

On the morning of Saturday, March 18, 1967, Captain Pastrengo Rugiati was asleep in his cabin when the message came down from the bridge: 'Bishop Rock 25 miles dead ahead.' It was around dawn and the rocky landmark west of the Scilly Isles was still out of sight. But it showed up on the radar.

On the bridge was First Officer Silvano Bonfiglia, who had been in charge of the ship and its Italian crew since Captain Rugiati had gone to his bunk at 2.30 a.m. During the night, as the ship had headed north towards England, it had been on automatic pilot. The route was supposed to be to the west of Bishop Rock. But when First Officer Bonfiglia checked the bearings at 6.30

93

a.m., he found that the ship was off-course. It was heading, not to the west of the Scillies, but to the east. The ship's bow was aimed straight for the treacherous 20-mile-wide channel that separates the Scillies from Land's End, Cornwall.

In good weather, most ships could pass through that narrow channel without danger. But not this ship – an oil tanker en route from Kuwait to Milford Haven, South Wales, with 120,000 tons of crude oil aboard. Nearly 1,000 feet long and with a 50-foot draught, this was one of the biggest ships in the world – the *Torrey Canyon*.

As soon as Bonfiglia realised the error, he took the tanker off automatic pilot and steered towards Bishop Rock. His plan was that the tanker should head for the rock for another hour, then change course to pass safely around it.

Having completed the manoeuvre, Bonfiglia telephoned the captain with the news. But, to his astonishment, Captain Rugiati countermanded the plan. Without coming to the bridge, he ordered Bonfiglia to alter course back again to the route through the channel. Bonfiglia did so, and put the *Torrey Canyon* back on automatic pilot.

Within half an hour, Rugiati had dressed and was on the bridge. After a conversation with another officer, Bonfiglia went off duty. At 8 o'clock, with the ship still 14 miles off the channel, the skipper adjusted his course once again so as to pass about six miles from the Scilly Isles. He was well aware of the danger of his action. For slap in the middle of the channel between the Scillies and Land's End are the Seven Stones, a group of rocks which through the centuries have been the graveyard of hundreds of ships. The Seven Stones are usually visible, but at high tide they are submerged. At mid-morning on March 18, 1967, the weather was fine, visibility good, the sea calm – and the tide high. If Captain Rugiati were as little as two miles out on his course, he could find himself right on top of the Seven Stones.

Shortly after 9 a.m. the crew of the lightship which guards the Seven Stones saw the *Torrey Canyon* approaching, heading straight for the mile-wide line of rocks. The lightship's warning flag was raised and rockets were fired. There was no response from the tanker.

Captain Rugiati may or may not have realised that he was heading for the rocks. It was his plan to veer to port as he entered the channel, and this he did. Still on the bridge, he took the tanker off automatic pilot, swung the bows round west until they were pointing due north, then switched back on to automatic. He was prevented from swinging further to the west by the presence of two fishing boats ahead of him.

The *Torrey Canyon* was still heading for the rocks – at its full speed of 16 knots. At the last minute, Rugiati realised that disaster was staring him in the face. He ordered his helmsman to go to the wheel and turn hard to port. The

helmsman swung the wheel round . . . but nothing happened. He called the captain and Rugiati realised that the wheel was ineffective because the steering was still on automatic. Rugiati switched to manual, and the tanker's bows began to swing around. But vital seconds had been lost. At 8.50, the *Torrey Canyon* hit the submerged Pollard Rock – the first of the Seven Stones – and stuck fast.

For a moment, Rugiati remained speechless. He realised that he had captained his giant oil tanker – difficult to manoeuvre at the best of times – at top speed and with no hand on the wheel straight on to a group of well-charted rocks. The captain sombrely demanded damage reports. The information he received was as bad as he could possibly have imagined. He knew that he had blundered – with disastrous consequences.

Worse was to come. . . .

0900 hours: The *Torrey Canyon* is fractured along half the length of its hull. Oil is pouring into the sea at 6,000 tons an hour from the ship's 23 full oil tanks. Rugiati orders an attempt to be made to regain buoyancy by jettisoning oil. He hopes that the tanker can be lightened to float itself off the rocks. The pumps start up and thousands more tons of oil flood into the sea.

1100 hours: A Royal Navy helicopter hovers over the *Torrey Canyon*. It is immediately clear to the helicopter crew that the oil pollution is on a scale unprecedented anywhere in the world.

1200 hours: The Dutch salvage tug *Utrecht* arrives on the scene. Salvage experts board the *Torrey Canyon* and estimate that the tanker is aground over three-quarters of its length.

1500 hours: Three further tugs and two ships of the Royal Navy arrive on the scene. The navy begin spraying the edges of the ever-growing oil slick with detergent. Meanwhile, in London, Ministry of Defence chiefs are ordered to Plymouth to set up emergency headquarters in the battle to combat the oil heading for West Country beaches.

2100 hours: 30–40,000 tons of crude oil have been pumped into the sea since 0900 hours. Now the pumps fail as the ship's boilers are flooded.

March 19: More Royal Navy vessels ring the *Torrey Canyon*, pouring detergent on to the growing oil slick.

March 20: The Royal Navy's chief salvage officer arrives on board, along

---

Amateur fire-eater Christopher Dawson swallowed too much turpentine and paraffin during his act. While driving home that night, he was stopped by police. Dawson, of Taunton, Somerset, failed a breathalyser test and was fined £100.

with agents of the American owners, the Union Oil Company of Los Angeles. The salvage men reckon that there is a reasonable chance of saving the ship, provided that the weather stays fine and the tanker does not break its back.

March 21: An explosion rips through the aft-superstructure of the tanker, killing the chief salvage officer of the Dutch team. There is a danger of further blasts, but work carries on. By now, all the original crew of the *Torrey Canyon*, except for Captain Rugiati and three officers, have been taken off by the lifeboat from St. Mary's, on the Scilly Isles.

March 22: Prime Minister Harold Wilson, who has a summer retreat on the Scilly Isles, orders a team of government advisers and scientists to go into emergency session to investigate all possible means of saving the coastline, its beaches and its wildlife from the drifting oil mass. Things look grim. A heavy swell has built up and it is now extremely dangerous to manoeuvre salvage craft alongside the *Torrey Canyon*.

March 23: The wind, which since the crash has remained north-westerly, increases in force to 20 knots. Twenty-four ships are now spraying detergent on the oil. Final preparations are made for attempting to refloat the *Torrey Canyon* on the high spring tides of March 26 and 27.

March 24: The wind changes to south-westerly – pushing the vast oil slicks straight towards the Cornish coast. Since the crash an estimated 50,000 tons of oil has been spewed into the sea. Aboard the *Torrey Canyon* there remain a further 70,000 tons.

March 25: The first oil hits the coast – thick, black and clinging. It builds up in layer upon layer on beaches, harbour walls, cliffsides and on the hulls of pleasure boats. And with the oil comes a pathetic flotsam – thousands of blackened seabirds, either dead or dying. Sixteen miles from the befouled coastline, three tugs attach lines to the *Torrey Canyon* in readiness for a trial pull. Air is pumped into the empty tanks to increase buoyancy, but the tugs only succeed in pivoting the vessel round on the rocks by about eight degrees.

March 26: It is Sunday, the first day of the high spring tides. Salvage men curse as a gale blows up, but by mid-afternoon the wind has abated slightly and four tugs strain to haul the giant tanker off the rocks. With a crack, and a frightening whiplash, the main cable linking two of the tugs to the tanker snaps. Minutes later, the tanker breaks its back on the rocks . . . spilling another

---

It is small wonder that morale is so low. Dentists, inadequately paid for their work, are pulling out in droves.
— *Freedom* (Scientology journal)

50,000 tons of oil into the sea. All attempts at salvaging the ship are abandoned. The disaster is complete.

March 27: The coastline from Land's End to Newquay, Cornwall, is black with crude oil. And it is only the beginning. Vast slicks are heading up the English coast – and equally enormous patches of oil are heading for the French coast. To make matters worse, the oil is drifting on to the beaches on the highest spring tides for 50 years.

March 28: The weather worsens, but an attempt is made to ignite the oil floating around the tanker. It fails. Captain Rugiati, his remaining crew and the salvage experts decide finally to abandon the tanker. The twisted hulk, washed by heavy seas, is breaking up. From the Defence Ministry in London, the order goes out: BOMB THE TORREY CANYON.

For the three days that followed, Buccaneer fighter-bombers of the Royal Navy rained bombs on to the oil tanker, which by now had broken into three parts. The pilots had to carry out their task with pinpoint accuracy. The decks of the ship had first to be opened up by the Buccaneers' 1,000-pounders, then the remaining oil below-decks had to be ignited.

The navy flyers did their job well: after the first four hits, the flames and smoke of the burning oil made it difficult, from a height of 2,500 feet, to aim further bombs on to the wreck, yet, of the 40 bombs dropped, 30 scored direct hits. To help keep the oil burning, Royal Air Force Hunter fighters flew over the wreck, jettisoning their wing-tip fuel tanks on to the inferno.

The following day, oil was still seen to be pouring from the wreck, so the Buccaneers and Hunters returned, firing rockets and dropping napalm and high-explosive bombs. Bombing continued on the third day, but no new fires were seen – the remaining oil had been burnt up.

There was plenty of oil still around, though – on the sea and on the beaches. On April 6 oil from the *Torrey Canyon* reached the Channel Islands. On April 9 it reached the shores of Brittany, and sixty miles of it, up to 12 inches thick, fouled the French coast. About 5,000 tons of oil had to be removed by an army of workmen. The last slicks were finally 'sunk' by the French Navy, using detergents in the Bay of Biscay in June – three months after the disaster.

In the meantime, a board of inquiry was held in Liberia, where the tanker was registered. Its conclusions were:

'The master alone was responsible for this casualty. It was his decision to pass to the east of the Scilly Isles. It was his decision to pass between the Scilly Isles and the Seven Stones. He made these decisions without consulting his officers and without any prior advice to them of his intentions. The board concludes that the master did not exercise sound judgement or exercise the practice of good seamanship. Nor can it be considered that he took proper action under the circumstances.

THE WORLD'S GREATEST MISTAKES

'The board considers that the master was imprudent in his decision to pass to the east of the Scilly Isles, instead of the west as originally intended. Considering the facts that the master's experience in the waters to the east of the islands was very limited and that the *Torrey Canyon* was an extremely large and deeply loaded tanker, his decision exposed his vessel to an unnecessary risk which could easily have been avoided.'

The board of inquiry criticised Captain Rugiati for failing to go directly to the bridge upon being told that the ship was off its original course. It also censured him for 'failing to reduce speed at any time prior to stranding' and for 'permitting his vessel to continue on automatic steering while nearing the Scilly Isles.'

Finally, the board reported: 'This casualty was one of the most serious nature. Apart from the loss of a fine ship and its cargo, the resulting oil pollution inflicted untold hardship and damage. It was one of the worst disasters in maritime history. The cause was entirely the negligence of the ship's master, and the degree of that negligence we consider to be of a very high order. A master charged with the responsibility for navigating one of the largest vessels in the world must exercise the care and caution which that responsibility demands. In this case, the master utterly failed to adhere to these standards. We recommend therefore that the licence issued to the master of the *Torrey Canyon* be revoked.'

Rugiati, a broken man, returned home to Genoa, where he went into hospital, seriously ill with pleurisy and suffering from depression. He would see no one but his wife and two sons. But soon, as the extent of his personal suffering became known, letters began pouring into the hospital at the rate of 200 a day. Most were letters of sympathy from people in Britain.

Rugiati eventually agreed to talk about the disaster. Friends were shocked when they met him. A shattered man, bent, grey, dazed, unshaven and trembling, he said: 'Those letters from England have given me back a little faith in myself. I am responsible for what happened and I have been suffering nightmares of guilt over it.

'The worst thing is knowing that I could have saved the ship if only I had had another 30 seconds to manoeuvre. As the ship was about to hit the rocks I tried to throw the helm. But it was on automatic and it would not respond. Nothing could be done.

'If only I had had another 30 seconds.'

Something no motorist should be without . . . The Self Grip Wench.

– Motor

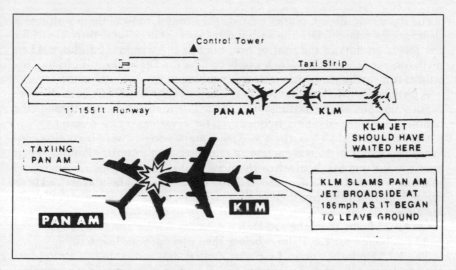

The world's worst plane crash

Two jumbo jets collided, and 582 lives were lost

It was the ultimate horror that everyone had dreaded – a crash between two jumbo jets loaded with passengers. It happened on March 27, 1977, on the Atlantic holiday island of Tenerife, in the Spanish-administered Canary Islands. And it claimed 582 lives.

The crash occurred on a Sunday, always the busiest day of the week at Santa Cruz. As many as 180 planes take off or land with their cargoes of holiday-makers. This particular Sunday was foggy – not unusual for Tenerife, where clouds bank up around the extinct volcano, Pico de Teide. There was also a great deal of confusion and extra traffic at Santa Cruz airport that day. A bomb, planted by terrorists of the Canary Islands liberation movement, had exploded in a shop at Las Palmas airport, on the neighbouring island of Gran Canaria, and aircraft were being diverted from Las Palmas to Santa Cruz. Among them were two Boeing 747 jumbo jets – Dutch KLM flight 4805 from Amsterdam and Pan Am flight 1736 from Los Angeles and New York.

By early afternoon, Santa Cruz airport was overcrowded even by its own hectic standards. Eleven planes were on the ground, most of them waiting for clearance for take-off. Dealing with the unexpected flood were three air-traffic controllers on duty in the control tower beside the terminal buildings. Their main concern was the fog, which was becoming thicker by the minute, and the central runway lights, which were not working.

A further problem was that two of the airport's three radio frequencies were out of action and all the waiting pilots had to talk to the controllers through the babble of the one remaining frequency. The scene was set for disaster.

On Pan Am flight 1736, the 370 American passengers were becoming restless. They had paid $2,000 each for a cruise starting from Las Palmas. Their liner was waiting for them when the news of the bomb explosion was passed to the aircraft and it was diverted to Santa Cruz. The holidaymakers had been sitting impatiently aboard their jet for two hours, unable to disembark because the airport did not have enough landing steps to go round.

On KLM flight 4805, the 229 Dutch passengers were also restless. They too had been bound for Las Palmas before their aircraft was diverted.

The KLM pilot, Captain Jaap van Zanten, was something of a celebrity. His handsome face had appeared in the airline's advertisements to underline the expertise of their staff and the safety record of their planes. Van Zanten was certainly experienced; he had been flying with KLM for 27 years and was one of its three most senior pilots. It was because of his experience that Van Zanten decided that he would not join the expected queue for fuel at Las Palmas airport when his and all the other craft were finally allowed into it, but instead would order his jumbo jet to be loaded now with the fuel that it would need – fuel that was later to incinerate the entire aircraft. . . .

Van Zanten's counterpart on the Pan Am jumbo was Captain Victor Grubbs, a 56-year-old veteran of World War Two. Unable to taxi around the refuelling Dutch aircraft to get ahead of it in the line of planes waiting on the runway, he tried to alleviate the boredom of his passengers by inviting them up to inspect the cockpit in groups.

By now, visibility was down to 500 yards – low, but still within the permitted limit for take-offs. The fog was thickening fast, however, and since no one

A big-selling vodka firm decided to drop its advertising line, which went: 'I thought the Karma Sutra was an Indian restaurant until I discovered Smirnoff.' An executive of the firm said: 'We conducted a survey and discovered that 60 per cent of people did think it was an Indian restaurant.'

relished the idea of being stranded at Santa Cruz overnight, the crews of the two jumbo jets were anxious to get clearance for their flights to Las Palmas.

The main runway at Santa Cruz is two miles long and 2,000 feet above sea level. It runs east to west. Parallel to it is a second runway which planes use to taxi to and from the terminal buildings. These two runways are joined at either end, and are linked along their lengths by four access slipways.

At a few minutes before 5 p.m., Van Zanten and Grubbs breathed sighs of relief when word came from the control tower that they should prepare their aircraft for take-off. Because of the congestion on the taxi-ing runway, both pilots were ordered to move their planes on to the main runway. The KLM and Pan Am jumbos arrived together at the eastern end of the main runway. The control tower then ordered the two jets to taxi westwards up the runway to the take-off starting point at the far end. They did so, with the KLM jet leading.

These manoeuvres went on largely out of sight of the three air-traffic controllers. Swirling sea fog blanketed the airport, and, because Santa Cruz had no ground radar, the controllers could not follow the pattern of slow-moving aircraft on the ground. They had to rely on that single busy radio channel.

The control tower radioed KLM flight 4805: 'Taxi straight ahead to the end of the runway and make backtrack.' Captain Van Zanten's mighty jet headed slowly up the long runway.

Captain Grubbs then received his instructions from the tower – to taxi forward and to leave the runway by turning into a slipway on the left.

The third turning to the left off the main runway at Santa Cruz airport is designated Slipway C3. It involves a 130-degree turn and leads straight back to the terminal buildings. It would have been a slow and awkward manoeuvre for the Pan Am jumbo. The fourth turning off the runway – Slipway C4 – leads in a circle to the top of the runway, where the KLM jumbo was now swinging around in readiness for take-off.

Captain Van Zanten completed his manoeuvre and pointed his airliner's nose into the darkening fog that hung over the two miles of main runway ahead of him – and over the Pan Am jumbo which, hidden from view, was still lumbering towards him.

The Pan Am jet passed the turn-off to Slipway C3 and headed on for Slipway C4. At about the same time, Captain Van Zanten's co-pilot was relaying this message to the control tower: 'KLM 4805 is now ready for take-off. We are waiting for clearance.'

Tower: 'OK. Stand by for take-off. I will call you.'

The tower then asked the Pan Am jumbo if it had yet cleared the runway. When told that it had not yet done so, the tower then asked the American co-pilot to report immediately the runway was clear. But moments later, the KLM plane began rolling. . . .

A jumbo jet weighs 240 tons, its wingspan is 195 feet, it is 231 feet long and its tailplane is the height of a seven-story building. At 5.07 p.m. on that fateful Sunday, two such planes were heading towards each other – one at a crawl, the other at 150 miles an hour.

Pan Am co-pilot Robert Bragg was the first crewman to spot the approaching Dutch jumbo. He said: 'I saw lights ahead of us through the fog. At first I thought it was the KLM standing at the end of the runway. Then I realised the lights were coming towards us.'

Bragg screamed: 'Get off. Get off.' Captain Grubbs shouted: 'We're on the runway. We're on the runway.'

Grubbs slewed his jumbo into a 30-degree turn to try to get out of the path of the oncoming airliner. But it was too late. The KLM plane was travelling too fast. It could not stop or swerve. It had passed the point of no return.

Captain Van Zanten lifted the nose of his jumbo at the last minute. A channel was gouged out of the runway by the Dutch plane's tail as the captain tried to leap his giant machine over the Pan Am jet. His effort was in vain. Two seconds after lifting off, the Dutch plane smashed into the American jumbo at about 160 miles an hour. The nose of the KLM jet hit the top of the other plane, taking the roof off the cockpit and the first-class upper compartment. The giant engine pods hanging beneath the wings were next to hit the American plane. The port engines ploughed into the aft-cabin, killing most of the passengers instantly.

The KLM Boeing continued its terrible journey over the top of the Pan Am plane and along the runway, disintegrating and exploding into thousands of pieces. Not one person aboard the Dutch plane survived.

All the survivors on the Pan Am plane were sitting either up front or on the left-hand side, away from the impact. Part of the left of the plane was broken off by the crash, and the survivors either were hurled clear or leaped to safety.

Throughout the long seconds of disaster, the air-traffic controllers remained unaware of it. A Spanish airliner flying above Tenerife broke in to request landing permission. The control tower replied sharply: 'Radio silence, please. I will continue to call up KLM.' But KLM no longer existed.

Suddenly, a gust of wind blew a gap in the fog. And those in the control tower had a momentary vision of horror as a blazing jumbo showed through the mists. A few seconds later another gap appeared . . and the controllers saw what remained of a second Boeing.

The radio waves became filled with a babble of voices. 'There's a jumbo on fire.' 'No, there are two of them.' 'Can you contact Pan Am 1736?' 'Control tower, have you seen fire on the runway?' 'Fire tenders, fire tenders.'

The small rescue team on duty at the airport was quickly at the scene. But there was little it could do. The KLM jumbo was an unrecognisable litter of scattered debris. The Pan Am jumbo was a blazing mass. Everyone who had escaped had done so within the first couple of minutes.

Heroine of the crash was Dorothy Kelly, a 35-year-old Pan Am purser from New Hampshire. This is what she remembered of the disaster: 'There was noise, things flying around. Nothing was recognisable. There was nothing around that looked like anything had looked before – just jagged metal and small pieces of debris. When everything settled, I realised that there was sky above me although I was still in what had been the aircraft. At first, I didn't see any people at all. There were explosions behind me and I realised that the only way out was up. The floor started giving way as I climbed out.'

Mrs. Kelly leaped 20 feet to safety then looked back at the broken and blazing plane. There was a string of explosions and she heard people screaming from within the aircraft – so she ran back towards it.

'I saw the captain on his knees, not moving. I thought he had broken his legs. There were other people around with broken limbs. I grabbed the captain under the arms and pulled and kept encouraging him to keep going. I feared the fuselage would fall down on us. There was a huge explosion. I said: "We've got to go now – faster." I kept pushing and pulling and then dropped him on to the runway.'

Mrs. Kelly had saved the life of Captain Grubbs. As explosions ripped the jumbo, she dashed back and forth, dragging other dazed survivors clear of the wreckage until she was certain that there could be no one else left alive. Later, Mrs. Kelly, her face scarred, her eyes blackened and with one arm in plaster, said: 'I feel as if I have just gone 20 rounds with Muhammad Ali.' She was subsequently awarded a medal for gallantry.

Pan Am passenger Jim Naik, a 37-year-old Californian, was in the first-

THE WORLD'S GREATEST MISTAKES

AUDIENCE TRIED TO SPOIL PLAY BUT PLAYERS SUCCEEDED

— Sunderland Echo

---

class compartment when 'all hell broke loose – just as if we were in a movie.'

This was Naik's story: 'I was sitting with my wife Elsie when there was a sudden explosion. The plane went completely up in flames. I was struggling to get Elsie out with me but after the impact people just started tumbling down on top of us from the lounge above as the ceiling caved in. A piece of ceiling fell on my wife. Then a second explosion hurled me on to the runway. I was running back towards the plane to try to save Elsie when I saw a body falling out of the plane. It was my wife.'

Briton John Cooper, a 53-year-old Pan Am mechanic, was travelling as a passenger on the flight deck when the plane was hit by the KLM jumbo. He was thrown clear and suffered only minor cuts. He said: 'There was a terrible crash. I just don't want to remember it. There were people screaming terribly – women and children enveloped in flames. I will never get the sounds of that screaming out of my ears.'

Californian John Amador, aged 35, said: 'I looked out of a porthole and saw the KLM plane coming right at me. I ducked and, when I looked up, our own aircraft was split into three parts. I was afraid I was going to be roasted.' But he leaped to safety.

So did Mrs. Teri Brusco, of Oregon. She said: 'The Dutch jet's wings took off the whole of the top of our plane. Everyone was screaming.' Her husband Roland pushed his wife through a jagged opening in the side of the plane and they then hauled out his mother. 'My mother was on fire. We started dragging her across the field to put the flames out.'

Several passengers remained strapped in their seats after the crash. They appeared numbed and did not try to save themselves. Then came the series of explosions that engulfed the plane in flames. Of the Pan Am jumbo's 370 passengers and 16 crew, more than 300 were dead within minutes of the crash and more than 60 were seriously injured.

But at least there were some survivors from the American jet. On the KLM jumbo, all 229 passengers and the crew of 15 were wiped out, including a Dutch wife who had boarded the flight at Amsterdam after telling her husband she was going on holiday with friends in Spain. Instead she flew off to her death – with one of her husband's best friends.

One further tragic lie came to light after the crash. A Dutch businessman told his wife that he was flying off to a company meeting in Switzerland. Instead, he boarded KLM flight 4805 for Las Palmas to spend an illicit holiday with an attractive woman neighbour. Before setting out, he had written a card to his wife and given it to a colleague to post from Zurich. The card, complete with loving greetings, arrived two days after his death.

And what of the man who set in motion the terrible chain of events of March 27, 1977? Antonio Cubillo, leader of the Canary Islands separatist movement, the man who ordered the bomb to be planted, said from his exile in Algiers: 'The Spaniards did not want holidaymakers to see the damage at Las Palmas. So it is their fault that the planes crashed. I do not have 582 deaths on my conscience.'

The shipwreck survivor who sacrificed his life in vain

The tiny liferaft was just a dot on the surface of the vast Pacific. Aboard it were Bill Quinlan, aged 48, and his 18-year-old nephew, David Lucas. David was reasonably hopeful that they would soon be spotted by a passing ship, but his uncle was despondent and morose. He blamed himself for the predicament they were both in.

Quinlan, a married man with two children, had set sail with his nephew from San Diego, California, on a 4,000-mile voyage to the Galapagos Islands. But after 1,000 miles their trimaran ran into a hurricane. A giant wave lifted the 40-foot yacht and smashed it upside down with the two occupants underneath it. They struggled to the surface, gasping for air, but Quinlan was soon back under the yacht again – trying to free the liferaft which was roped to the deck. It took him an hour, but he made it.

The next task was to rescue fresh water and rations from the cabin. Quinlan was beneath the yacht again and Lucas was holding the end of a rope attached to his uncle's waist, when the young man saw a giant black fin slicing through the water. Blood from a cut on Quinlan's leg had attracted a shark.

Lucas hauled on the rope and dragged his uncle back on board the liferaft. The raft began drifting away from the trimaran as the shark circled them. The two survivors knew that they would have to make do with the meagre rations they already had.

The storm receded, and the blazing summer sun – it was July, 1978 – beat down on the little raft. It was well away from the main shipping routes, and the men aboard it lay drifting for five days without once sighting another vessel.

Quinlan took stock of the emergency supplies. There was one can of water and two cans of food. He spoke softly to his nephew: 'God alone knows how long it will be before someone spots us. There is enough food and water here to keep one man going for two weeks. You are only 18. You have a full life ahead of you.'

And with those words, Quinlan slid over the side of the raft.

Lucas grabbed his uncle and tried to haul him back but Quinlan, the stronger of the two, struggled free and began, with steady strokes, to swim away from the raft. He never once looked back.

'I shouted for him to return,' Lucas said later. 'I cried but he never looked round. I didn't know what to do. I cannot swim and I could only watch him vanish out of sight. I saw sharks in the water and I knew he was as good as dead. I'm sure I will never again meet anyone as brave as my uncle.'

But Quinlan's heroism was in vain. The very next day, a Mexican fishing boat picked up Lucas. His rations were untouched.

When he was put ashore, Lucas travelled north to Arcata, California, to the home of his uncle's wife, Vicki. There he handed over the only two possessions left by Quinlan – a gold ring and a tin on which was the scratched message: 'I love you. I'm sorry.'

Hydrogen bombs rain on Spain

Bomber crash threatened nuclear catastrophe

A giant U.S. Air Force B-52 bomber kept its rendezvous with a flying tanker over the Mediterranean coast of Spain at 10.20 a.m. on January 16, 1966. The cargo of the B-52 was four 1.5-megaton hydrogen bombs, and the plan had been circling over the eastern Mediterranean for 12 hours. Now, the bomber had to take on fuel in mid-air from the tanker before flying back to the United States.

Aboard the B-52, the captain took up position 20 miles behind the tanker at 30,000 feet. It had been a long and boring mission, no different from the

American soldiers and Spanish police guard the wreckage of bomber and tanker.

100 bomber flights made by U.S. Strategic Air Command along the Iron Curtain borders every day of the year.

Aboard the K-135 tanker ahead, Major Emila Chapla kept a steady course as he watched the bomber manoeuvre into position behind him. Earlier, Chapla had taken off from the U.S. airbase near Seville, Spain, with more than 30,000 gallons of aviation fuel aboard. It was just a routine, everyday job.

The B-52 closed the distance, ready to fit its nosepipe into the fuel boom that trailed from the underbelly of the tanker plane. Chapla watched the B-52 drift closer. He thought it was approaching too high and too fast. He gave a radio warning to the B-52, but his urgent words had only just been uttered when the two huge aircraft collided. The B-52 came up under the tanker and hit its belly.

Major Chapla fought to control his severely damaged plane and to return it, blazing, to base. In the B-52, the captain knew that his aircraft was doomed. The superstructure and the cabin were crushed, and the plane began to break up. The captain and two of his crew baled out – just before a tremendous explosion, which set the giant bomber spinning earthwards, shedding thousands of fragments on its way.

Amidst the debris that rained down on the Spanish coast that morning were four 20-foot-long hydrogen bombs.

The bombs fell in the vicinity of the village of Palomares. None of them exploded. That would have been impossible without their having first been primed aboard the B-52. But it was feared that their casings might have been split open by their TNT detonators exploding on impact, and no one knew for sure what effect leaking radio-active plutonium and uranium would have on the unsuspecting civilian population of Palomares.

THE WORLD'S GREATEST MISTAKES

As soon as the crash occurred, a military disaster team was assembled and flown from the United States to Spain. Meanwhile, American military advisers in Spain broke the news to the Madrid authorities, and a stream of top brass and politicians poured into Palomares.

A bald statement was issued to the press to the effect that an American plane had crashed but that there had been no civilian casualties. No mention was made of the nuclear weapons. The peasantry of Palomares were unaware of the dangers that surrounded them. But, with the arrival of the American disaster team and the unprecedented security clamp on the area, newspapermen began putting the clues together. They discovered that the crashed plane was a B-52. They guessed that it had been carrying nuclear bombs, and that those bombs were now scattered over rural Spain.

Piece by piece, the newsmen put together the jigsaw of the disaster, even though they were barred from the area. The outside world was told in huge headlines what was going on around Palomares. But in the village itself the peasants were told nothing. They were barred from harvesting their crops and were ordered to remain in the village. As troops and search planes swarmed over their farmlands, the 2,500 people of the Palomares district became increasingly alarmed.

If they had known what danger they were in, they would have been even more inclined to panic. For the three bombs which had fallen near their village had all been split open by their detonators, spilling plutonium and uranium into the atmosphere. The slight breeze blowing that day was wafting an invisible poison across the dusty Spanish countryside.

The first bomb to be recovered was spotted in open fields by aerial searchers. The TNT explosion had blown out a small crater, and the shattered casing was partly buried in the earth. There had been little leakage. Another splintered bomb was found in hilly countryside about three miles out of Palomares.

A third bomb was found by a villager close to his home on the outskirts of Palomares. It was in a small crater and smoke was coming from it. Not only smoke but, unknown to the villager, radio-active dust. The puzzled Spaniard examined the shattered bomb, stood on top of it and gave it a kick. He went off to look for someone who might know what the mystery object was, and it was only after some hours that word got to the Americans that a bomb had been found.

Three bombs accounted for . . . but where was the fourth?

Fisherman Simo Orts provided the answer. He had been out in his boat when the air crash occurred 30,000 feet above him. Some minutes later he watched a long metal object sink slowly out of the sky beneath two parachutes. It fell into the sea only yards from his boat and quickly sank. Orts circled the spot but all traces of the mysterious object had disappeared. He continued

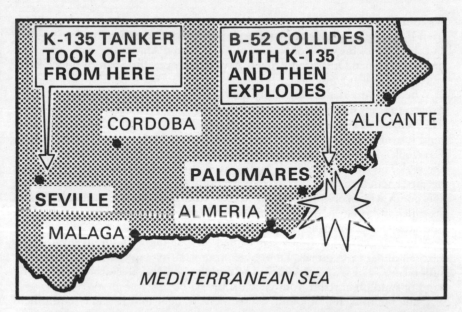

K-135 TANKER TOOK OFF FROM HERE

B-52 COLLIDES WITH K-135 AND THEN EXPLODES

CORDOBA

ALICANTE

PALOMARES

SEVILLE

AL MERIA

MALAGA

MEDITERRANEAN SEA

A villager washing clothes in Palomares.

his fishing, then set sail for home. When he arrived back in port, he told his friends about the strange occurrence. They decided to inform the local police. But, because of the cloak of secrecy thrown by the Americans over what they had code-named Operation Broken Arrow, not even the Spanish police knew exactly what was going on.

When the Americans eventually heard of the fisherman's tale, they sent out experts to track down and interrogate the puzzled Orts. His description fitted. The bomb had fallen into the sea suspended beneath a parachute designed to hold it over a target area. The second parachute had been the safety 'chute. Orts took a team out in his boat to show them exactly where the bomb had hit the sea. The trouble was that, once out in the Mediterranean, he could not be sure enough to pinpoint the spot exactly. All the searchers knew was that the bomb was likely to be somewhere within a ten-square-mile area about six miles offshore, where the craggy seabed ranged in depth from between 100 and 5,000 feet. Somewhere down there was the fourth bomb.

A marine search party was assembled off Palomares, with 20 ships, 2,000 seamen and 125 frogmen. There was also a bathyscaph and two miniature submarines. The team was ordered to find the bomb at all costs before drifting sand or mud obscured it from view on the seabed.

If the bomb were not found, there was a danger that its safety equipment might in time rust away, allowing the radio-active contents to pollute the Mediterranean – or even causing an explosion that would create a deadly nuclear cloud over the coast of Spain. There was also the possibility that, if the bomb were abandoned, the Russians might try to find it and unravel its secrets. The bomb *had* to be found.

And found it was. On March 15, two months after the air crash, the crew of the mini-submarine Alvin spotted an indentation in the mud at 2,500 feet. They investigated more closely, resurfaced – then, agonisingly, failed to find it again. A day later they picked up the trail and discovered a parachute on the seabed. They followed the ropes of the 'chute . . . and there, on a narrow ledge overhanging a 500-foot precipice, lay the bomb.

It took a further three weeks to secure the bomb without dislodging it from the ledge. But on April 7, 1966, after several near-disasters, the hydrogen bomb was raised undamaged to the surface. Meanwhile, the people of Palomares had been largely cleared of the danger of contamination, and compensation was being agreed for the loss of crops.

A nuclear tragedy on an unthinkable scale had been averted.

Deep-freeze meat: Best Scotch beef from Wales.
– Glasgow Herald

Death of the Red Baron

German air ace tempted fate, and flew to his death

In the heat of the battle for the air during World War One, at a time when a pilot's life expectancy was three weeks, young flyers on both sides guarded themselves with lucky charms and surrounded themselves with superstition. Among the German pilots of the string-and-canvas flying machines, one superstition was held to be more important than all others: not to be photographed

before a mission. Only afterwards, would they allow a camera to record their victories.

On the morning of April 21, 1918, Baron Manfred von Richthofen, the deadliest ace that air warfare has ever known, laughed at the superstition. He paused to play with a puppy at the door of the hangar which housed his bright red Fokker triplane, and he smiled into the lens of a camera held by a visitor to the airfield.

Baron von Richthofen could afford to laugh at superstition. After all, at the age of 25, he was the most famous flyer in the world. He was considered almost invincible. The day before, he had shot down his 80th aircraft. He was a national hero, known as the Red Knight of Germany and the Red Baron, because of the 'flying circus' of blood-red planes that he led twice a day into the skies over war torn France and Belgium to wreak havoc among British, French, Australian and Canadian aircraft.

Richthofen stepped into the cockpit of his Fokker at 10.15 that morning as a military band played in honour of his victories. He took off from the airfield at Cappy with two dozen other planes and flew towards the village of Sailly-le-Sec, in the Somme valley, where they were to assemble.

At about the same time as Richthofen was bumping down the take-off strip, another pilot was preparing for take-off 25 miles away, at Bertangles. He was Roy Brown, a 24-year-old Canadian who flew a Sopwith Camel with 209 Squadron of the newly formed Royal Air Force. Brown, a volunteer flyer from Toronto, was very unlike the flamboyant Red Baron, whom he was shortly to meet in combat. Retiring and modest, he had notched up 12 official German 'kills' – certainly less than his actual tally, because he seldom bothered to claim his victories. Brown had recently been promoted to captain and had been awarded a Distinguished Flying Cross. He was flying two long and dangerous missions every day of the week and was keeping his tired body going by regular infusions of brandy and milk.

Brown had heard much about Baron von Richthofen and had learned to respect the pilots of his amazing 'flying circus'. Richthofen, on the other hand,

---

It can be a mistake to cross swords with the great wits of the age. In Georgian days a Member of Parliament indignantly broke off from his speech in the House of Commons and said: 'The Prime Minister is asleep.' Lord North opened one eye and said: 'I wish to God I was.'

Lady Astor once told Sir Winston Churchill: 'If I were your wife, I'd put poison in your coffee.' Churchill replied: 'And if I were your husband, I'd drink it.'

had never heard of Captain Brown, the man who, at 11.15, was flying 10,000 feet above him, one of a flight of 15 RAF planes, over Sailly-le-Sec.

Below him, Brown saw the mighty circus attacking two slow RE8 reconnaissance planes which were wheeling, twisting and turning in an attempt to escape the onslaught. Brown flipped his Camel into a steep dive and, by arrangement, seven of his colleagues followed suit. Eight was about the most of their battle-scarred squadron that they could risk committing to the fray. As they roared down towards the dogfight being enacted at 3,000 feet, they knew that they were heavily outnumbered by the Germans and that one of the eight who were joining battle was really only along for the ride. He was Lieutenant William May, an Australian who had just arrived in France and had been ordered to keep on the edge of any dogfight until he had gained more experience. May circled the mêlée and watched as the seven other Camels engaged the German planes – allowing the two beleaguered RE8s to flee into a bank of cloud.

The outnumbered RAF pilots were amazingly successful. Within a matter of minutes they had downed four of the German planes, one being shot down by new boy May. But no sooner had May sent the enemy aircraft to the ground than Baron von Richthofen himself swooped down to line the Australian up in his sights. The Fokker's twin Spandau machine-guns raked the fuselage of May's plane. The Australian received only a minor injury but he was in serious trouble. Try as he might, he could not shake the Red Baron from his tail. He spun and wheeled, but he was too inexperienced to outmanoeuvre the German ace.

Brown saw what was happening and disengaged from the dogfight. May was now making a determined run for home, his plane low to the ground, the Baron only 25 yards behind him. With the advantage of height, Brown swooped down until he had caught up with the German. An Australian battery opened fire on Richthofen's plane, but the Baron kept determinedly on.

So intent was he on his prey that the victor of 80 air battles forgot the very first rule in the book of aerial warfare: always look behind. Brown was right there on his tail, his right thumb hovering over the trigger button of his Vickers machine-gun. The Red Baron came into his sights and Brown opened fire –

Pilot Douglas Corrigan took off from New York in dense fog in 1938, planning to fly west to California. Unfortunately he got his bearings wrong and flew due east for 28 hours. He landed in Ireland and gained the nickname 'Wrong-Way Corrigan'.

---

one long burst which sent a neat line of bullets along the Fokker's fuselage, starting at the tail and running up to the cockpit.

The nose of the Fokker dipped and the plane glided earthwards. It hit the ground and rolled neatly to rest near the British lines on the outskirts of Sailly-le-Sec. A British soldier looked into the cockpit and found Baron Manfred von Richthofen sitting bolt upright, dead. An officer took a snapshot of the scene, to be dropped over the German lines the next day.

Meanwhile, back at Cappy airfield, a German photographer was watching the sky. He was awaiting the return of the 'flying circus', so that he could take his second photograph that day of the ever-victorious Red Baron.

The mutineers who sailed away to death

The three new recruits to the crew of the sailing ship *Leicester Castle* were a surly bunch. They had joined the British cargo ship at San Francisco, though whether by choice is not known. For this was 1902, and, although press gangs no longer roamed the streets of the world's major ports, there were other devious methods of obtaining crew members for long and hazardous voyages – such as getting them roaring drunk and leading them aboard the ship just before it sailed.

Not that Captain John Peattie, master of the *Leicester Castle*, would personally have had anything to do with such deception. The tough Scotsman would have left all that to his first mate. All Peattie knew was that there were three new crew members for the voyage back to London, and that was that. The three were James Turner from Oregon, Jack Hobbs from Illinois and Ernest Sears from Idaho – all ordinary seamen who had served previously on ocean-going vessels.

The three Americans kept their own company. But they did ask a lot of questions about the ship's route. And when on August 12 they were told that the ship was passing to the north of the Pitcairn Islands, in the middle of the Pacific, the reason for their questions was made plain.

Turner, Hobbs and Sears had decided to desert. They had lashed together some timber to make a rough raft, which they had hidden in the hold. And just before midnight, they put their plan into action.

Sears knocked on Captain Peattie's cabin door and asked the master to come to the saloon immediately to help tend a crewman who had been injured on deck. Peattie followed Sears down the passageway and entered the saloon – to be confronted with Hobbs armed with a revolver. The Scot made a dive for the gunman but Sears smashed a length of wood down on his head. As Peattie lay on the floor, Hobbs fired four bullets into him.

The only man on watch that night was another Scot, the young second mate, Iain Nixon. Hearing the shots, he rushed down to the saloon and was shot through the heart with a single bullet. He fell dead in the doorway.

The captain, however, was still alive. One bullet had missed his heart by inches, the others had hit him in the arm and shoulder. The whole of the ship was awake now and, while some of the men tended the captain's wounds, the others dashed up on deck to find the attackers.

They were too late. Sears and Hobbs, along with their friend Turner, were crouched on their makeshift raft drifting away into the darkness of the Pacific.

The mutineers had taken with them only a few days' supply of food and water. They were obviously heading for the Pitcairn Islands – there was no other landfall that they could have contemplated.

The three men were clever enough to have worked out that the faint breeze then blowing would move their raft slowly towards the islands. But it did them no good. For when the other crewmen had told them that the *Leicester Castle* was passing the islands, they had been only partly right. No one aboard except the captain and the first and second mates knew that the lack of wind had caused them to sail 300 miles to the north of the Pitcairns.

The three mutineers were swallowed up by the endless Pacific. They were never seen again.

Nobody believed the Subbay family, of Cherbourg, France, when they claimed that their clock was jinxed. The old grandfather clock sometimes struck 13 instead of 12 – and when it did, the unlucky number was always accompanied by an accident. When the head of the household first heard the 13th chime, he fell downstairs. On another occasion his wife scalded herself and, like her husband, had to be rushed to hospital. A sceptical relative moved into the house so that he could disprove the jinx. At the 13th stroke of midnight a heavy lamp standard fell on his head and he too was rushed to hospital.

The £12 million air giant that ended in a scrapyard

In 1942 the aircraft factories of Britain were turning out bombers as fast as they could build them. But despite the pressures of war, there were still dreamers around. And most of them seemed to have been gathered in one room in London's Whitehall, where a committee headed by air pioneer Lord Brabazon was deciding the future of the British aircraft industry.

What these wise men proposed was that work should start on a giant airliner that could fly halfway around the world – one that could carry passengers from London to New York non-stop. It would cost a lot of money to build, and there was no spare money during the war effort. It would use valuable factory space, and there was none of that spare either. Nevertheless, in March 1943, the decision to build two prototypes of this giant plane – called the Bristol Brabazon – was announced in Parliament. It was to be the prestige aircraft of the century. And the word went out: money no object.

The planemakers at Filton, near Bristol, needed no prompting. They designed a plane that was to be the biggest in the world – a fantastic 70 tons

Above The Bristol Brabazon on its first trial flight. *Right* Lord Brabazon.

empty and 140 tons laden, with a 230-foot wing span, 50 feet high and with engines developing 20,000 horse-power.

They built a brand-new hangar in which to assemble the prototypes. They extended the runway at Filton by demolishing most of the village and by concreting over a new main road. They built a ridiculously lavish full-scale mock-up of the aircraft, complete in every detail, even down to the soap dish in the women's powder room. Passengers? Well, they could fit about 75 of them in, with sleeping berths, bars and promenades – this at a time when the Americans were already building 150-seat aircraft.

At the end of 1949, seven-and-a-half years after Lord Brabazon's report, the first Bristol Brabazon made its maiden flight at Filton, watched by the world's press. The flight was a success. But six months later it was discovered that the flying giant was suffering from metal fatigue. It was cracking up. Its operational life would be about two years.

In September 1952, the House of Commons was told that the Bristol Brabazon was being scrapped. The cost of the project had been £12½ million. Only one plane had ever been completed. The biggest airliner in the world was sold for scrap for £10,000.

Chapter Three

Victims and Villains

For every man with money, there is another scheming to relieve him of it. For every man with a trusting nature, there is another ready to make him a little wiser. When the gullible discover that they have blundered, it is usually too late. In the pages that follow you will meet people who have paid dearly for one simple mistake.

The Great Train Robbery

How the perfect crime became the great foul-up

AUGUST
3
1963

I t was high summer in the heart of the English countryside. The date was August 3, 1963, the place Bridego Bridge at Sears Crossing, Buckinghamshire – the setting for a crime that was to capture the world's imagination and to become known as the Great Train Robbery.

It was shortly after three o'clock in the morning on that August day that 15 men loaded 120 mailbags into a lorry after robbing the Glasgow-to-London night mail train. The mailbags contained £2½ million.

The Great Train Robbery was almost the perfect crime. Almost. For due to a monumental blunder, it turned into a disaster that made the villains who pulled off the robbery the most notorious criminals in the world.

The plan for the raid was hatched in January 1963. It all began with a meeting between a London solicitor's clerk and Gordon Goody, one of the leading lights of a South London 'firm' of criminals. The rendezvous, cheekily enough, was the most famous court in the land, the Old Bailey. There, the clerk boastfully confided to Goody that someone he knew had information about where a vast sum of money could be 'lifted'.

Goody was interested. He called in his friend, Ronald 'Buster' Edwards. And through a string of contacts and secret meetings over the next few days, the incredible project was outlined to them.

Every night, according to the informants, old banknotes from all the banks in Scotland were sent by train to London to be destroyed. The money was always in what was called the High Value Packages Coach which formed part of the night mail train from Glasgow to Euston. There were usually five Post Office workers in this coach, which was always next-but-one to the diesel engine. The other coaches further down the train were manned by dozens of mail sorters. But the coach next to the engine contained only parcels. It was unmanned. The amount of money being carried in the High Value Packages Coach varied from day to day but always rose dramatically after a bank holiday. On August 6, for instance, it might be as much as £4 million. The problem was how were they to rob the train?

However the job was to be tackled, Goody and Edwards realised that it was going to be too big a task for them alone. Through the spring of 1963, the gang grew as more and more tough and specialised criminals were recruited. The team even included members of a rival 'firm' then operating in London.

The gang contained a colourful bunch of villains. Principal among them were: Goody, a tough 32-year-old loner with a sharp taste in clothes and girls; Edwards, aged 30, an overweight but likeable club owner who was a devoted family man; Bruce Reynolds, also 30, married but fond of high living; Charlie Wilson, 32, a resourceful criminal friend of Reynolds; Jimmy White, a quiet, 49 year-old ex-paratrooper; Bob Welch, 34, a South London club owner and one of the top men in the second 'firm'; his friend Tommy Wisbey, a 32-year-bookmaker; and Jim Hussey, aged 30, who ran a restaurant in London's Soho.

The gang also brought in three specialists: 'wheel man' Roy James, 23, a silversmith and racing driver, winner of several major races; Roger Cordrey, a 38-year-old florist who was an expert at 'adjusting' railway signalling equipment; plus a retired train driver. At the last minute, they also recruited a small-time thief and decorator, with a pretty wife, an engaging smile and a yearning for the luxury life he could never afford. His name was Ronald Biggs.

Bridego Bridge carries the main Scottish railway line over a winding back road through Buckinghamshire farmland. It was at this spot that the gang had decided to rob the train. By August 2, they had all assembled at a large and lonely farmhouse, Leatherslade Farm, 26 miles from the bridge. They were dressed in an assortment of commando gear. They decided that it would be a good cover if they looked like soldiers out on a night exercise. To complete the picture, they had two Land-Rovers and a lorry painted army green.

At around midnight, these motley 'soldiers' of fortune set out from the farm

---

The career of outlaw Jesse James ended in a shoot-out at Northfield, Minnesota, in 1876. The gunfight began when a bank cashier refused to open a safe. One of the James gang fired at the cashier, alerting the townsfolk who put the bandits to flight. It was later discovered that the safe had not been locked.

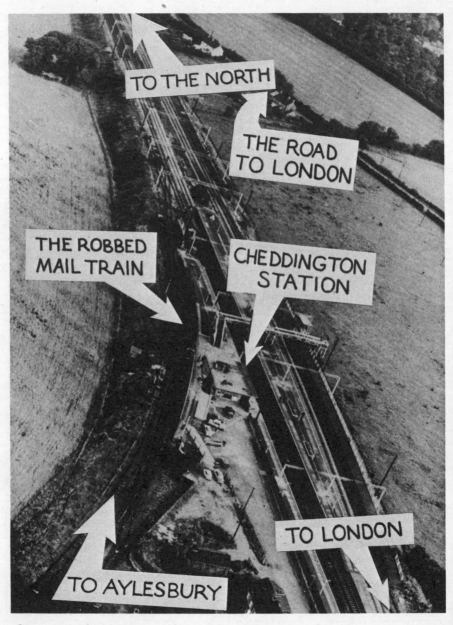

TO THE NORTH

THE ROAD TO LONDON

THE ROBBED MAIL TRAIN

CHEDDINGTON STATION

TO LONDON

TO AYLESBURY

in convoy and drove to Bridego Bridge to prepare the amazing ambush. They were armed with pickaxe handles, coshes and an axe to break down the door of the coach. Cordrey, the diminutive rail-equipment fixer, organised the switching of the two warning lights – one several hundred yards up the track and another closer to the bridge. The first warning light, sited beside the track, would cause any train to slam on its brakes. The second, on a gantry above the line, would bring the train to a full stop. The gang also cut the lines to trackside emergency telephones and to nearby farms and cottages. Then they waited.

The train was due to come into view from the bridge at 3 a.m. The timing had been checked night after night on dummy runs by the gang. On the morning of August 3 it was right on schedule. The look-out man alerted the rest of the gang by walkie-talkie, and they all took up positions on the embankments beside the line.

On the train, driver Jack Mills looked out for the usual green trackside light. But tonight it was amber. He put on the brakes and throttled back the mighty diesel. The overhead signal gantry came into sight. It was showing a red light. Mills stopped the train directly under it and asked his fireman, David Whitby, to use the emergency telephone beside the gantry to find out what was going on.

Whitby vanished into the darkness. Mills heard him ask someone: 'What's up, mate?' Then nothing. Whitby had encountered Buster Edwards walking down the track, had asked his innocent question – and found himself bundled down the embankment and pinioned to the ground by some of the burliest, most villainous-looking thugs he had ever seen.

Back in the cab of the train, driver Mills was being attacked from both sides. He kicked out at the men trying to climb up into the cab but he was overpowered from behind and hit twice across the head. Blood poured down his face, and the next thing he remembered was being handcuffed to fireman Whitby.

The gang had got their train but they still had not got at the money. The next step was to separate the engine and the two front coaches from the rest of the train and drive the engine forward from the gantry to Bridego Bridge, where the cargo was to be unloaded.

The 'heavies' in the gang then launched themselves against the High Value Packages Coach. With axe, crowbar and coshes, the door and windows were smashed in, and the five petrified Post Office workers inside were suddenly faced with what must have seemed like the advance force of an army. The postal workers were made to lie down on the floor while the gang unloaded the mailbags through the shattered coach door and along a human chain which led down the embankment and into the back of their lorry.

Then, sweating but jubilant, the gang drove back in their military convoy to Leatherslade Farm. The operation had gone exactly according to plan, but for the knock on the head received by driver Mills. In time, it proved to be a big 'but' – for the violence used against him weighed heavily at the robbers' trial, and his death some years later brought claims from his family that his health had deteriorated dramatically after the raid.

But, for the moment, as the mailbags were piled up in the living room of Leatherslade Farm, the future for the gang looked rosy. They spent the rest of the night counting out the money. They set aside sums for major bribes and backhanders, and shared out the rest. In all there was £2½ million.

Years later, in a remarkable book about the robbery*, Goody related how he had sat with a bottle of whisky in his hand listening to the police wavebands on his VHF radio. He heard one policeman tell a colleague: 'You're not going to believe this, but someone's just stolen a train.'

The gang members had all concocted their alibis and made arrangements to salt away their shares of the loot until the hue and cry was over. They left the

* *The Train Robbers* by Piers Paul Read (W. H. Allen, the Alison Press and Secker & Warburg, 1978)

The mail train at Bridego Bridge, the pick-up point for the lorry.

farm and went their separate ways brimming with confidence. It was short-lived. . . .

Most of the gang had left damning evidence behind them at Leatherslade Farm. There were fingerprints, clothing and vehicles. But the robbers had not been over-worried. They had arranged for an associate to stay at the farm after they had moved out and to clean it from top to bottom so that not even a hair from their heads would be found if the police ever searched the place.

The job was never done. The contract was bungled. The 'perfect crime' became the ultimate criminal foul-up.

When the police found the farmhouse hideout, most of the robbers went on the run. Detectives knew who they were from the fingerprints and palm prints they had left. One single Monopoly board was a mine of information to forensic scientists. Soon the faces of the robbers were on posters all over Britain.

Within a year of the robbery, most of the gang were in jail. The 30-year sentences which were meted out for 'a crime against society' shook the thieves – and even created a measure of public sympathy for them. Goody, Welch, James, Wisbey and Hussey all got 30 years, although they were eventually released after serving 12 of them. Cordrey got 14 years and was freed after seven. But the robbers who gave police the most trouble were Reynolds, Buster Edwards, Wilson, White and Biggs.

With his paratrooper's training, White went on the run in England, taking with him his wife and baby son. He evaded capture for three years but, with his money stolen or blackmailed from him by 'friends', he was almost glad to be caught. He was captured while working as an odd-job man on the Kent coast, and in 1965 was jailed for 18 years. He eventually served only nine of them.

Reynolds and Edwards also evaded arrest, even though their names and faces were known to every policeman in Britain. They hid out in London for almost a year, then fled with their wives and children to Mexico City. Edwards even underwent plastic surgery to alter his appearance. But their money was being spent at a frightening rate and their life as exiles began to pall.

Both eventually returned to Britain. At the end of 1966 Edwards gave himself up to police. He was given a 15-year sentence and served nine years. Reynolds was arrested in Torquay, Devon, in 1968 – five years after the robbery. Chief Superintendent Tommy Butler of the Flying Squad knocked on the door of the Reynolds' home at 6 o'clock on a November morning and said: 'Hello, Bruce – it's been a long time.' Two months later Reynolds appeared in court and was sentenced to 25 years in jail. He was released in 1978.

Life in prison was never easy for any of the train robbers. They were all kept under the closest security because of two sensational escapes. Wilson was sentenced, along with the rest of the gang, to 30 years' imprisonment in 1964.

He remained in jail for just one year. He escaped, with outside help, from Winson Green Prison, Birmingham, and joined Reynolds and Edwards in Mexico City. But, like his friends, he tired of the place and settled down under a false name with his wife and three daughters in a smart suburban home near Montreal, Canada. But early in the morning of January 25, 1968, Chief Superintendent Tommy Butler arrived at the front door. Behind him, and surrounding the house, were 50 men of the Royal Canadian Mounted Police. Wilson was flown back to England to continue his 30-year sentence. He was also released in 1978.

Apart from the few members of the gang who had never been caught and convicted, the arrest of Wilson and Reynolds and the surrender of Edwards left only one man still wanted by the police – Biggs, the small-time crook who had been lured by the glittering promise of the crime of the century was sentenced to 30 years' jail along with Goody and the rest. In July 1965 he was out of prison again – 'sprung' by an armed gang who broke into London's Wandsworth Prison. He fled to Australia with his wife and children. But later, with the police not far behind him, he moved on to Brazil, leaving his family in Melbourne.

Early in 1974 a reporter of a London newspaper tracked down Biggs and set about writing his story. Unbeknown to the reporter, however, the newspaper's executives had tipped off Scotland Yard about the scoop they were about to break. As a result, on February 1, 1974, Chief Superintendent Jack Slipper and another police officer arrived in Rio de Janeiro to arrest Biggs.

The former Train Robbery Squad officer was soon given a new title by the British press: Chief Superintendent Slip-up. For Brazil had no extradition agreement with Britain, and the Rio police refused to hand over Biggs. Then Biggs's young Brazilian girlfriend announced that she was pregnant. The father of a Brazilian child could not be deported. After his much-publicised swoop, Slipper flew home empty-handed. And the last – though probably the least – of the Great Train Robbers went free.

Police in Venezuela issued a warrant for the arrest of a known criminal. Unfortunately for them, the man's house was built slap across the Venezuela-Colombia border.

When they called to arrest him, he ran into his bedroom, locked the door and phoned his lawyer. The bedroom was in Colombian territory, and the offence with which he was to be charged was not punishable in that country.

The Venezuelan police gave up.

Hans van Meegeren.

Kings of the art forgers

Fake 'Old Masters' have fooled dealers and even museums

Brimming with confidence, David Stein walked into the shop of a well-established New York art dealer one afternoon with three water-colours under his arm.

The dealer stood back and admired them. He carefully studied the certificates of authentication and was impressed by the signatures on them – 'Marc Chagall'. There was some discussion over money, and a cheque for $10,000 was handed over.

Both men parted happily – the dealer because he had bought the paintings so cheaply, Stein because he had got rid of three more fakes.

Those three 'Chagalls' had not even existed seven hours before. Stein had awoken in his New York apartment at six o'clock that morning and remembered that he had an appointment with the dealer at one in the afternoon. So he had decided to get down to a bit of quick forging.

He had 'aged' three sheets of paper with cold tea. Then, after dreaming up suitable subjects, he had polished off the three paintings without a break. He had rushed out to have the paintings framed and, while waiting, had written himself three certificates of authentication. Then he had gone off to keep his appointment with the dealer.

That day's forgeries had been in the style of Chagall, but they could equally have been based on the work of a dozen artists from Renoir to Gauguin. Stein could turn his hand to them all. And that is where he went wrong.

'If only I had stuck to dead men,' he lamented later. For at the very time that he was selling his three fake water-colours, Chagall was in New York. The Russian-born artist had arrived to see two of his enormous murals erected in the Metropolitan Opera House. The dealer had an appointment to visit him, and he took along the three paintings to show the old artist. Chagall took one look at them and declared: 'Diabolical.'

The police came for Stein that same night. 'They arrived at the front door, and I left through the back with a glass of scotch in my hand,' he said. Stein fled to California, where he was arrested and decided to confess all.

The four-year reign of Stein, king of the art forgers, was at an end. The suave, sophisticated, 31-year-old man-about-town spent 16 months in a New York jail after being indicted on 97 counts of counterfeiting and grand larceny. While inside, he helped the police to form an art-forgery squad.

When he came out of jail in 1968, Stein, who was half-British, half-French, decided to put all such risky ventures behind him. He said goodbye to his three American galleries, his New York apartment and his art earnings of up to $500,000 a year, and returned to Europe. Unfortunately, he did not realise that further charges were awaiting him, and he was sentenced to two-and-a-half years in a French prison.

By the time he came out again, Stein was famous throughout the art world. His bogus Old Masters were much sought after. But he decided to paint and

---

Railway staff at Wolverhampton station picked up from the platform a note which had been thrown from the window of a passing train.

It read: 'Mr. Russell, of 32 Vale Road, Bloxwich, Staffs, has left the kettle on the stove. Please inform the police.'

The police, duly informed, called at Number 32 to find the kettle on the stove but the gas unlit.

David Stein signing one of his paintings with others in the background.

sell his own works in his own style. He was instantly successful, and set up homes and businesses in Paris and London.

Stein remained bitter about the people he saw as the real fakers – the pretentious phoneys of the art world.

'People who buy a painting and find out that they have made a mistake are angry because they have displayed their own ignorance,' he said. 'About two or three hundred of my works are still on the market as originals. I see them in dealers' catalogues, in salerooms and even in museums. A lot of the art world is fake.'

Just how much of the contents of museums and art galleries is fake, and just how much is genuine, we shall never know. The art forgers are just too clever for most experts.

America's Cleveland Museum of Art had to remove from display one of its most prized possessions, a wooden Madonna and Child, supposedly carved in Italy in the 13th century. In fact, it was carved around 1920 by an Italian art restorer, Alceo Dossena. His fake was only discovered in 1928 when the sculpture was X-rayed and modern nails were found to be imbedded in the wood.

The museum put the Madonna and Child in its basement and looked around for other works to replace it. Three weeks later it bought a marble statue of Athena for $120,000. It too was a Dossena fake.

In 1918 the New York Metropolitan Museum of Art paid $40,000 for a seven-foot statue of an Etruscan warrior which had supposedly been buried since pre-Roman days. One arm of the warrior was missing, as was the thumb of his other hand.

In 1960 Alfredo Fioravanti confessed to the museum that he was one of six men who had created the statue between them 50 years earlier. He produced the warrior's missing thumb to prove it. The thumb fitted perfectly.

In 1975 the same museum had to withdraw from display a beautiful 'Greek' bronze horse when it was shown to be a fake. The horse had been one of the museum's most popular attractions.

Among the most renowned art forgers of this century was the hard-drinking Dutchman, Hans van Meegeren. His exploits came to light after World War Two, when he was put on trial for helping the Nazis. He had sold to Hermann Goering for $150,000 an exquisite painting purporting to be by the Dutch master Vermeer.

Van Meegeren's answer to the charges of complicity made against him was that he had not sold a Vermeer but a Van Meegeren. The painting was a fake – and it was only one of dozens that he had sold for vast sums around the world.

At first, the judge did not believe him. But he gave the painter a chance to prove his boast. Van Meegeren was placed under guard in his Amsterdam studio and told to paint another Vermeer that could fool the experts. He did so, and was freed.

The master forger's freedom was short-lived, however. As more and more Van Meegerens came to light he was brought to trial again – this time on a charge of deception. He was jailed for 12 months, but died before he could complete his sentence.

Even the grand old master Michelangelo is reputed to have raised much-needed funds as a struggling young man by selling to a Rome cardinal a statue of Cupid which the artist had first stained and buried to age it into an 'antique'.

Perhaps the most prolific forger of sculptures was Giovanni Bastianini, who, before his death in 1868, turned out terracotta busts by the dozen under contract to an art dealer. They were considered to be perfect examples of Renaissance sculpture, and the Florentine faker's works appeared in museums around the world. There are still two in London's Victoria and Albert Museum.

In 1977 a beautiful wooden carving of a kneeling stag was given pride of place in the antiques department of Harrods, the department store in London. It was reputed to have come from a French château and to have been carved around 1580. The price tag was £9,800.

Then Frank Sedgwick, a 47-year-old ex-fitter whose hobby was woodwork, walked into the store and said: 'That's mine.'

What was claimed to be a fine example of 16th-century craftsmanship had been knocked up by Sedgwick in a fortnight. He had carved it five years earlier at his home in the Kent village of Petham and had sold it for £165. It had changed hands several times since, and each time its antiquity and its price had grown – until Harrods accepted it for sale. After Sedgwick's visit, they removed it.

Famous faker Clifford Irving (see page 144), the American author jailed for his forged biography of Howard Hughes, once wrote another biography, entitled *Fake*. It was about the exploits of a stateless Hungarian, Elmyr de Hory, whose paintings have hung in dozens of galleries around the world.

The book reported that De Hory's paintings were among millions of dollars'

In 1928, Liberian President Charles King put himself up for re-election. He was returned with an officially stated majority of 600,000 votes. King's opponent in the poll, Thomas Faulkner, later claimed that the election had been rigged. When asked to substantiate his allegations, Faulkner pointed out that it was difficult to win a 600,000 majority with an electorate of less than 15,000.

THE WORLD'S GREATEST MISTAKES

> **The Reverend Edgar Dodson, of Camden, Arkansas, chose for a sermon the theme 'Thou shalt not steal'. While he was preaching, someone stole his car.**

worth of fakes sold to a Texan millionaire. The ensuing scandal made De Hory famous, although he says firmly that he had never tried to pass his work off as someone else's: that is, he has never put a famous signature to one of his own paintings, even when that painting has been in the precise style of a sought-after artist.

In 1974, at the age of 60, De Hory was taken from his home on the island of Ibiza and put into jail in Majorca. There was no formal charge, and he was out again after four months.

Like so many with his talents, he never disguised his contempt for the international art pundits who 'know more about fine words than fine art'. He claimed he could paint a portrait in 45 minutes, draw a 'Modigliani' in ten, and then immediately produce a 'Matisse'.

'The dealers, the experts and the critics resent my talents,' he said, 'because they don't want it shown how easily they can be fooled. I have tarnished the infallible image they rely upon for their fortunes.'

Even distinguished experts of the most famous art gallery in the world, the Louvre, in Paris, have been taken for a costly ride. The gallery's worst blunder was revealed in 1903 when a Parisian painter claimed that he was the creator of one of its most treasured possessions – a beautifully intricate golden head-dress called the Tiara of Saitaphernes.

The claim was untrue. The tiara was a fake, sure enough. But the man who had made it was not the Parisian painter. Its creator was a Russian goldsmith, Israel Rouchomowsky – and he did not want the false claimant to take credit for his work. So Rouchomowsky travelled to Paris to put the record straight. The administrators of the Louvre continued to deny that the tiara was a fake, until the old Russian produced the original designs he had drawn for the headdress eight years earlier – and, to rub salt into open wounds, began working on a new tiara, as intricate in every detail as that in the Louvre.

In the Louvre today hangs what must be the best-known and best-loved painting in the world. It is also one of the most copied. It is the Mona Lisa. In 1911, the famous smiling lady was stolen. Three thieves, dressed as workmen, had walked casually into the gallery before it shut one evening and had hidden in a basement room. The next day, the Louvre was closed for cleaning. The 'workmen' wandered into the hall where the painting was hung, took it off the wall and walked out of the gallery carrying it, frame and all.

VICTIMS AND VILLAINS

Of the three men, only one had been in this line of business before. He was Vincenzo Perugia, an Italian burglar. The other two were art forgers Yves Chaudron and Eduardo de Valfierno, who had developed their forgery techniques in South America. There, they would interest a crooked dealer or collector in a particular painting at a gallery and promise to obtain it for him, at the right price. The two would then present themselves at the gallery as art experts and take the painting down in order to study it. They would then produce an exact copy, attach it to the back of the genuine painting, and invite their prospective buyer to the gallery to put his mark surreptitiously on the back of the canvas. Later they would remove the fake from the original and take it to the client. There, on the back of the canvas, the buyer would see the mark he had made – the 'proof' that he was getting the genuine article.

In each case, the gallery experts were none the wiser – they still had their original – and the buyer, when he discovered he had been tricked, could hardly complain to the police.

Chaudron and Valfierno switched their operations to the world's art capital, Paris. There, they went one stage further with their elaborate deceptions. They printed phoney pages of newspapers, which included stories about valuable paintings having been stolen. They would show the stories to gullible collectors and then sell them forgeries of the 'stolen' works.

Finally, the tricksters decided that they were ready for their biggest coup. They would forge the Mona Lisa. But this time they would make sure that the buyers would never later be confronted by the genuine article and discover they had been tricked. For this time Chaudron and Valfierno would steal the original.

They recruited Perugia into their gang and, within months of pulling off their amazing robbery, they had forged six Mona Lisas and sold them to gullible Americans for $300,000 each.

Chaudron and Valfierno still had the genuine treasure hidden, but whether they planned to destroy it, sell it, or even return it, will never be known. Their accomplice, Perugia, stole it from them and fled to Italy, where he clumsily tried to sell it himself.

The gang were uncovered and the Mona Lisa was returned to the Louvre, where, under heavy guard, behind a thick glass panel, and surrounded by electronic alarms, it remains today.

STRIP CLUBS SHOCK.
MAGISTRATES MAY ACT ON INDECENT SHOWS.
                                                    – Daily Mirror

---

Was an innocent man hanged?

He was executed for a murder to which a mass-strangler confessed

In March, 1953, a prospective tenant was looking over the ground-floor flat of a decaying terraced house at 10 Rillington Place, in Notting Hill, London, when he detected a foul smell which seemed to be coming from a papered-over kitchen cupboard. What he found made him rush to the nearest telephone box and dial the police.

When they arrived, they stripped 10 Rillington Place. In the kitchen cupboard they found the bodies of three prostitutes. The bodies of two more women were found buried in the backyard. And beneath the sitting-room floor was the body of the wife of the previous tenant – a quiet, bespectacled man, Reginald Christie.

Christie and his wife, Ethel, had taken the flat 15 years earlier. None of their neighbours were aware that he had been convicted for five criminal offences – one of them an assault on a woman. During the war he applied for a job as a reserve policeman, and, because his record was never checked, he got it. After the war he worked briefly in a factory, then took a job as a Post Office clerk.

His neighbours thought him hard-working and respectable, although not particularly likeable. They often took his advice on medical matters, of which he pretended a knowledge. It was also rumoured that he could help a girl terminate a pregnancy.

After the discovery of the bodies in his former flat, Christie confessed to the murders. In one of the most sensational and horrifying trials in British history, it was said that he could gain sexual satisfaction only with dead women. Christie hoped to be found guilty but insane and that his life would be spared. But he was sentenced to death.

That, however, was far from the end of the story. For Christie also confessed to murdering the wife of an ex-neighbour, Timothy Evans. Evans, who had been hanged three years earlier for the murder of his baby daughter, had also confessed to the murder of his wife.

How was it that both men confessed to the same murder? To this day, no one knows for certain which of the two men killed Beryl Evans. But what is certain is that, but for the most tragic oversight in forensic history, no jury could possibly have convicted Timothy Evans of the crime.

His confession was made on the spur of the moment when he walked into a police station in Merthyr Tydfil, South Wales, on November 30, 1949, and told the officer at the desk: 'I would like to give myself up. I have disposed of the body of my wife.'

Evans, a gullible, illiterate van driver who was largely under the spell of the evil Christie, told detectives that they would find his wife's body in a drain at 10 Rillington Place, where the couple had occupied the top-floor flat.

When police arrived at the house, they could not find the dead woman in the drains. But a later search did reveal the body – in a small wash-house at the back of No. 10. She had been strangled – the same means of death meted out by Christie to all of his victims. But more shattering still was the discovery of a second corpse in the wash-house. It was the pathetic body of Evans's baby daughter, Geraldine.

Evans appeared to be broken by the discovery of his dead daughter. He at first admitted both murders, but later retracted his confessions and at his trial accused Christie of the crimes. He said that his wife was pregnant for the second time, and that Christie had offered to give her an abortion. Evans had agreed and left the two together. Afterwards, Christie had shown Evans his

---

Scott Brant was out walking near his home in Minnesota one night when he saw two eyes glowing in the dark. What he thought was a puppy loped over, licked his hand and snuggled up to him. Scott took it home, gave it a meal of hamburgers and milk and let it roam around his house. But he became worried when the animal began tearing his furniture to pieces, and he phoned a vet for advice. The vet called up the local zoo, which immediately sent two keepers along to recover their lost four-month-old lion cub.

wife's body and said that she had died during the abortion. He advised Evans to get rid of all his wife's clothing and other possessions and to leave London for a while. Meanwhile, Christie would arrange for little Geraldine to be adopted by a couple he knew.

That was Evans's story, but the jury did not believe him. In court, Christie, the ex-policeman, was a much more convincing witness. His previous conviction for viciously assaulting a woman was not mentioned. The prosecution described him as 'this perfectly innocent man'.

The simple-minded Evans was convicted – technically for the murder of his baby only – and hanged. Christie stayed free for another three years, in which time he committed another four murders before he was brought to justice.

Then, the furore over the Evans case began.

Despite the evidence that there had been a ghastly miscarriage of justice, it was not until 1966 that pressure for an official review of the case succeeded in prompting the government to authorise an inquiry under Mr. Justice Brabin. He ruled: 'It is more probable than not that Evans killed Beryl Evans, and it is more probable than not that Evans did not kill Geraldine.'

It was not the sort of verdict that the pro-Evans campaigners had fought for over the years. But it did mean that Evans, whose conviction was for killing his daughter, could receive a posthumous royal pardon. His body was exhumed from Pentonville Prison and reburied in consecrated ground.

Officially at least, guilt for the murder of his wife still rests with Evans, even though Judge Brabin's verdict of 'more probable than not' would never warrant a conviction in court.

But many questions remained unanswered. How could the detectives of the Metropolitan Police have failed to turn up the evidence that would, right from the start, have pointed the finger of suspicion at Christie? How, when investigating Evans's allegations, could they have failed to take serious note of Christie's five previous criminal offences? How could they have so firmly ruled out any involvement by Christie in the disposal of Beryl Evans's body simply on the basis of his assertion that fibrositis prevented him from lifting heavy weights?

Security staff at the Fifth Federal Reserve Bank in Richmond, Virginia, held a conference to discuss ways of making employees safer from attack following a spate of armed robberies. An argument broke out among the security men, and in the ensuing gunfight one guard was killed and three injured.

Above left Timothy Evans. *Above right* John Christie. *Below* Police at 10 Rillington Place.

> Scotland's national poet Robert Burns died from
> rheumatic fever in 1796. He might well have lived longer if
> his doctor had not prescribed daily baths in the muddy and
> freezing waters of the Solway Firth.

One other indication that police investigation might have been less than usually thorough was that on the first and second visits they made to 10 Rillington Place to search for the body of Mrs. Evans, they did not even take a look into the wash-house. It was only on the third visit that they made their grisly discovery. And then only after standing with Christie in his backyard and discussing with him the possibility of digging up his tiny garden to find out whether Beryl Evans was buried there.

If they had decided to dig up the yard, they would have found the shallow grave of, not Mrs. Evans, but two other women who had been lured to the house, strangled and buried by Christie.

As they chatted to Christie on that chill December morning in 1949, the detectives were standing on top of the bodies of the two women. While the men spoke, Christie's small mongrel dog dug with its paws at the earth around their feet – and uncovered a woman's skull. Christie shooed the dog away and kicked earth over the evidence. The detectives did not notice.

The next time the skull was uncovered was when Christie's backyard was dug up and the whole of 10 Rillington Place was pulled apart after the mass-killer's arrest in 1953.

By then, Timothy Evans – and four more women – were dead.

The gendarme and the lady driver

Young Jacques Piret was the newest, greenest cop on the beat. He had just qualified as a fully fledged policeman in Toulouse, France, and he was out alone on his beat in the centre of the town.

Piret had been warned about Evelyne Laforge. She was an attractive boutique owner who always parked her car outside her shop and who had already collected dozens of parking tickets – all of which she threw away without paying.

> **LUCKY MAN SEES PALS DIE.**
> – Headline from the *Baltimore News-American*

That morning, Piret spotted the delectable Mme Laforge stepping into her illegally parked car, so he hurried across the street to reprimand her. The young policeman had hardly begun to tick her off in the mildest terms when Mme Laforge started crying, then screaming, then throwing her arms around in a tantrum.

Piret squirmed in his police-issue shoes as a crowd gathered to watch the show. The embarrassed gendarme threatened to take the sobbing woman to the police station, but the cries only grew louder and the mood of the spectators angrier.

Finally, Piret told Mme Laforge that he would drive her home in her car. When they arrived at her house, she apologised and invited him inside for a drink while they sorted out the problem of the unpaid parking fines.

One drink followed another, and the gentle cop was still in the house when Mme Laforge's husband, Philippe, arrived home from work. Monsieur Laforge found his wife flustered and only half-clothed in the bedroom. He threw open the wardrobe door . . . and there was Piret, dressed only in his underclothes and with his neatly folded uniform in his arms.

The outraged husband made a grab for Piret. Mme Laforge screamed. Piret fled through the house and, as he did so, drew his revolver and fired a shot into the air to frighten off his pursuer. Then he dashed out of the front door and down the street, still dressed only in his underwear.

The biggest day in the life of Gendarme Piret had ended in disgrace. He later appeared in court and was fined £50 for 'outraging public decency'. And a police inquiry resulted in his being dismissed for 'wrongful use of his firearm'.

As the judge who fined him said: 'It was a classic case . . . Gendarme Piret was carried away by an excess of zeal.'

> **Cyril Prescot parked his car on a hill in Williton, Somerset, and walked to a nearby telephone box to phone a friend. Suddenly, another car came round a bend, and side-swiped Prescot's car, releasing its brakes. Prescot's car rolled downhill and crashed into the telephone box, knocking it over with him inside. The injured man was later treated for bruises and shock. He would have received medical attention sooner, but he was too dazed to remember to dial for help.**

Multi-millionaire Howard Hughes.

The Howard Hughes hoax

Publishers paid a fortune for an autobiography that never was

Hey, listen to this ... I've just had a wild idea.' The words were spoken by author Clifford Irving as he drove to a bar near his home on the Mediterranean island of Ibiza. Irving, crouched behind the wheel of his battered grey Simca, excitedly outlined to his friend Richard Susskind the idea for the publishing coup of the decade – the autobiography of the richest eccentric in the world, the legendary Howard Hughes.

If only they could get Hughes to talk, however briefly, they would have done what no one else had dared to try, and make themselves rich and famous into the bargain.

In fact, they failed to speak to the multi-millionaire. And the only coup that Irving pulled off was something quite different from the publishing coup of

'Biographer' Clifford Irving.

> **Pauline Jenkins had a 'hell of a shock' on her wedding night when she discovered that her husband was a woman. 'I threatened to leave there and then,' she said. 'But I went downstairs and made a cup of tea instead.'**
> *– News of the World*

the decade – it was the publishing hoax of the century.

Because Hughes would not speak to him, Irving did the next best thing he could think of. He wrote Hughes's autobiography himself, inventing most of it and lifting the rest from published material on Hughes.

Irving's logic was simple. Hughes was ageing, sick, possibly drug-addicted and, most important of all, a fanatical recluse who would allow no one near him apart from the small bodyguard of Mormon male nurses who cared for and protected him in a succession of hotel-suite hideaways around the world. If Hughes wished to challenge anything anyone wrote about him, he would have to appear in a courtroom. And Hughes would never break his long years of hermit-like existence to do that.

So what was there to stop Irving from making up his own Hughes 'autobiography', with reams of 'quotes' from the multi-millionaire, and selling it for a fortune?

Irving had always been a romantic, his imagination outrunning his moral scruples. Born in New York in 1930, he went to art college, where he displayed a slight talent – a talent that, many years later, was to equip him for the role of forger. He graduated from Cornell University in 1951 and announced that he was off to see the world. An incurable adventurer, he sailed the Atlantic, lived with California's beatniks and Kashmir's drop-outs, and ended up with his slim, blonde wife Edith living and writing on the fashionable Spanish island of Ibiza.

The publishers of Irving's books were McGraw-Hill of New York, and they looked after him well. They advanced him money when he ran short and they gave him help and encouragement when his efforts seemed to be flagging. It was to McGraw-Hill that Irving turned when he came up with his 'coup'.

Irving wrote to the publishers telling them that he had sent a copy of one of his earlier books to Hughes for his comments. The recluse had replied – and the author had quickly followed up with an offer to 'ghost' his autobiography. Surprisingly, Hughes had agreed. Would McGraw-Hill be interested?

McGraw-Hill certainly were interested, and the deal was struck. Hughes was to get a payment for allowing a series of tape-recorded interviews. In addition, hefty advance payments were to be made to Irving.

The whole lot – money for Hughes and advances and expenses for Irving – added up to about $1½ million. And it went straight into the author's pocket. It was frittered away by Irving and his friend Susskind on lavish holidays and junketing in Europe, the Caribbean and Central America. Wherever Irving went, he claimed to be fixing secret meetings with Hughes or his associates. In reality, he was staying at the best hotels, eating the best food, dining with the most beautiful women – and spending money as if it were going out of fashion.

Over the months, he countered inquiries from McGraw-Hill by pointing out Hughes's pathetic insistence on secrecy. And he cleverly kept his publishers interested – and quiet – by sending them sample manuscripts, letters apparently signed by Hughes, and tantalising details of the recluse's private life.

The manuscripts contained, quite simply, lies – quotations supposedly transcribed from fictional tape-recordings made by Irving in conversation with Hughes. But cleverly intertwined with these outright lies were half-truths and rumours embroidered from newspaper cuttings.

The letters signed by Hughes were really written by Irving to himself. But so clever were the forgeries that, when McGraw-Hill showed them to New York's leading handwriting analysts, they endorsed them as Hughes's.

The details Irving gave in memos about the recluse's private life were the only elements of fact in this otherwise great work of fiction. But these hitherto unpublished revelations did not come from Hughes's own tongue, or even from Irving's own researches. They were lifted from the memoirs of a former Hughes aide, Noah Dietrich. These memoirs, which Dietrich had been

Edith Sommer-Irving, wife and accomplice of Clifford Irving.

planning to turn into a book of his own, were secretly 'borrowed' by Irving, who milked them of some of their more interesting anecdotes.

The picture that Irving and Susskind had so far built up of Hughes was a dramatic one. According to Irving's information, the recluse was a far more glamorous character than the self-tortured misanthrope everyone imagined him to be in the last few years of his life. For instance, according to Irving, Hughes had flown secret missions from Britain during World War Two, had had a long and close friendship with novelist Ernest Hemingway, with whom he shared adventures and reminiscences, and, even during his silent years, was globe-trotting the sun-spots of the world having fun and games. All nonsense, of course, but just the material to make the book sell. McGraw-Hill were eager to publish.

The publishers kept pouring the money into Irving's pockets. The cheques that they made out to Hughes were quickly soaked up from the Swiss account in which they were deposited. The account, in the name of H. R. Hughes, had in fact been opened by Edith Irving using a passport forged for her by Clifford.

The goldmine suddenly ran out in 1971. By the most phenomenal coincidence, someone else had been dreaming up the same plot as Irving, and a rival publishing house announced that an official autobiography of Hughes was on its way.

Panic reigned at McGraw-Hill, as it did at the offices of the Time-Life organisation, who had agreed to buy the serialisation rights of the Irving book for a vast sum. Irving tried to confuse the issue by producing a new forged letter from Hughes demanding extra money for the final tapes and denouncing the rival book as a fake. McGraw-Hill once again fell for Irving's bland assurances of his sincerity – but they themselves had to announce the existence of their own Hughes autobiography for the first time.

The fat was in the fire. The Hughes organisation arranged a press conference at which reporters who had followed the saga of the billionaire recluse over the years were invited to put questions to Hughes himself over a direct telephone link. At the same time, Swiss banking authorities were investigating Edith Irving, alias 'Helga Hughes', who had drawn so much money out of the H. Hughes account in Zurich.

A man who had been deaf in one ear from the age of three was eventually cured when he changed his doctor. The man, a factory worker from Bridgwater, Somerset, was being examined by his new doctor when a cork popped out of his right ear. He said: 'I must have put it there when I was a child.'

Irving held out for as long as he could. But his lies and denials were finally seen for what they were when beautiful Danish singer Nina, once famous as part of the husband-and-wife folk duo Nina and Frederick, revealed that at a time when Irving claimed he had been meeting Hughes, the author had really been with her.

Irving confessed. Susskind, the man who had helped him set up the literary hoax of all time, was jailed in New York for six months. Irving was fined £4,000 and sentenced to two-and-a-half years in prison. His wife was sentenced to two years and a similar fine.

Clifford Irving maintained his remarkable sense of romantic melodrama right to the end. After hearing Edith sentenced, he sobbed: 'I have put my wife in jeopardy. She has suffered terribly. I have heard her cry herself to sleep at night.' Then he began planning yet another money-making project – a book about his $1½ million super hoax.

And the man whose fabulous wealth made all these dreams of avarice possible? Hughes died on a jet between Mexico and Texas in 1976, with the full story of his mysterious life still untold.

The man they couldn't hang

Aseries of blunders allowed John Lee to cheat the hangman and live out his life in peace. For Lee has gone down in history as the man they could not hang. Three times, murderer Lee stood on the newly built scaffold at Exeter Jail on February 23, 1885 – and three times the trap-door failed to open. Each time, Lee, 19, was taken back to his cell, engineers inspected the trap-door, the executioner pulled the handle, and, without Lee on the scaffold, the mechanism worked perfectly.

Lee had his death sentence commuted to life imprisonment. He was released after 22 years and later emigrated to America, where he died.

The theory for Lee's amazing good fortune is that when prisoners were helping to build the new scaffold they nailed a warped board underneath the planking. This board was beneath the spot where the chaplain stood while the prisoner was on the scaffold. The chaplain's weight would press out the board so that its end would cover the end of the trap-door and prevent it from opening.

Each time the engineers tested the trap-door they blundered in not having someone on the warped board where the chaplain had stood.

The £32 million 'mouse'

Lowly clerk gambled away a giant bank's assets

Few people in the world of high finance had heard of Marc Colombo. There was no reason why they should have done. He was just one of 59,000 names on the payroll of Lloyds Bank, a lowly foreign-exchange dealer in the Swiss backwater of Lugano.

But in September 1974, Colombo hit the headlines all over the world in a way that left hard-headed money experts open-mouthed in amazement. Lloyds Bank International announced that 'irregularities' at Lugano, the smallest of their 170 overseas branches, had forced them to suspend both Colombo and branch manager Egidio Mombelli – and had cost the bank a staggering £32 million.

It was the biggest loss ever announced by a bank in Switzerland, and a loss unprecedented in the history of British banking. The news wiped £20 million from Lloyds' London shares and left their top officials in despair over the loophole that had allowed it to happen.

What had the handsome 28-year-old wheeler-dealer been up to? And how had he got away with it?

Colombo was a little man with big ideas. He watched as the world's leading currencies daily changed their values on the foreign-exchange market, offering enticing opportunities for men shrewd and brave enough to buy when the price was right and sell at a profit. He decided to grab a piece of the action for his bank.

The 1973 Middle East War and the subsequent Arab oil embargo had sent exchange rates haywire, and Colombo was convinced that the dollar would lose value against the strong, stable Swiss franc. So, in November 1973, he plugged into the international phone network of money dealers and struck what is known as a forward deal.

He contracted to buy 34 million U.S. dollars with Swiss francs in three months' time. If, as he expected, the dollar was worth less when the time came to settle, he could buy back his francs with cheap dollars. But the dollar's value did not tumble. It went up. And Colombo lost seven million francs on the deal – about £1 million. A lot of money to a £9,000-a-year clerk, but not a lot, he reasoned, to a bank which had just announced half-year profits of £78 million.

Colombo, who had worked at the branch for less than a year, knew that reporting the loss to his boss, Mombelli, would probably get him the sack.

So he decided to increase his stake, and go for double or nothing.

So he began an amazing gambling spree. Without Lloyds suspecting a thing, he used their name and risked their money to set up transactions totalling £4,580 million in just nine months. At first, he was betting that the dollar would lose value. It did not. So he switched to gambling that it would go on rising. It did not.

In most offices, a checking system would soon have put a stop to Colombo's antics. Because most foreign-exchange deals are by phone, they are difficult to monitor, so confirmation in writing is usually sent to a third party at the contracting dealer's office. This ensures that holdings of different currencies can be balanced and risks minimised.

But Lugano had a staff of only 16, and no one, including Signor Mombelli, suspected that Colombo was anything other than a diligent, honest employee.

Colombo continued making deals he was not authorised to make with banks he should not have been dealing with. He was blatantly ignoring the £700,000 daily limit on debts or holdings laid down by head office. He was not covering his gambles on buying with counter-balancing orders to sell. He was using inter-bank swap arrangements to borrow cash to cover up losses. And instead of declaring his transactions in records sent to head office and the Swiss authorities, he was logging them in his diary.

Such madness could not go on forever, and the day of reckoning came in August 1974. A senior French banker mentioned casually to a Lloyds man in London that Lugano 'has reached its limit with us'. Alarm bells began ringing at Lloyds' offices in Queen Victoria Street. A phone check with a German bank revealed that it, too, had had massive unauthorised deals with Lugano.

Top executives left London secretly next morning. Unannounced, they confronted Colombo, Mombelli and Karl Senft, the man in charge of all three of Lloyds' Swiss branches. They seized all the papers they could find and flew back to London with the three Swiss employees.

Painstakingly, officials worked all weekend, unravelling the intricate and costly web Colombo had woven. To their horror, they found that he had contracted speculative forward deals worth £235 million which were still unpaid. And he had not hedged his bets. He had committed the bank to

> A Louisiana firm was given an old mattress to renovate. The workers had already thrown away and burned a lot of the old stuffing when they came across $20,000 hidden in the remainder. They returned this money to its forgetful owner; the other $6,000 he had hidden they had burned.

risking a sum 'largely in excess of the combined capital and reserves of all three banks in Switzerland'. Yet the official ledgers showed deals worth only £36,000.

With special permission from the Governor of the Bank of England, Lloyds transferred huge sums of money to Lugano to cover the promises Colombo had made. Then the bank's international money market director, Robert Gras, spent three weeks trying to minimise the damage – secretly, for any leak would have made the delicate operation more difficult and expensive. It was a mammoth task. When at last the books were in order, and all debts had been settled, Lloyds had lost £32 million.

When the bombshell news was announced by chairman Sir Eric Faulkner, Colombo and his wife had fled their luxury villa on a mountainside above Lake Lugano. Mombelli too had disappeared on an 'extensive holiday'.

But a year later they were both in court in Lugano, facing charges of criminal mis-management, falsification of documents and violations of the Swiss banking code. Colombo admitted exceeding his authorised dealing limits and conducting transactions with unauthorised banks, but denied accepting illegal commissions and criminal intent.

The prosecution described Colombo as the mouse that made Lloyds tremble, and accused him of gambling wildly like a man at a casino. He replied: 'Being a foreign-exchange dealer is always a hazardous operation. It is a gambler's profession.'

When questioned about how his losses had snowballed, he said: 'There was the pride of the foreign-exchange dealer who will not admit failure. I was at all times convinced that I could recoup my losses, but it only takes a little unforeseen something to upset the market. I was a prisoner of events.'

Mombelli, 41, made no secret of the fact that, all along, he had not really understood what was happening. He had initialled papers without realising their significance. The judge described him as 'a disaster, a bank manager without brains'. But Mombelli said after the trial: 'It's a foreign-exchange Mafia. For every dealer you need at least four administrators to check what he is doing. They do things that no ordinary banker understands.'

Lloyds in London were astonished when the two men walked free from the

---

In accordance with his usual custom, an unknown benefactor walked into the Church Army offices, handed over a cheque for £500 and left without waiting for thanks.

As large numbers of these parasites are around at this season, it may be useful to give some hints as how to exterminate them.

– *Western Daily Press*

---

court. Colombo was given an 18-month suspended sentence and Mombelli one of six months, and they were fined only £300 each, because the judge accepted that they were not lining their own pockets.

Colombo's only motive seems to have been to boost his own ego. Even if his wheeler-dealering had ended in profit, he would still have faced dismissal for unauthorised use of the bank's money. And a profit, after all, had not been an impossible dream for the young Colombo. . . . He later claimed that if his deals had been allowed to stand they would, through later developments on the foreign-exchange market, have netted Lloyds Bank £11 million profit.

Dirty works afoot

Sexually explicit literature fills the bookstores of Australia, as it does those of most major nations of the world. But it is not so long ago that a severe literary censorship operated in the country.

Within the present era, for instance, even posters simply portraying Michelangelo's classic nude statue of David were seized in a police raid on an Australian bookstore. And there have been as many as 5,000 books at a time on the country's 'banned' list, among them Aldous Huxley's *Brave New World*, Ernest Hemingway's *A Farewell To Arms* and Daniel Defoe's *Moll Flanders*.

But the petty purges on 'licentious' literature were on one occasion shown up for what they were. The law was made to look an ass by blundering into an elaborately laid hoax.

It happened in 1944 at a time when censorship was at its most oppressive. Arousing police suspicion in that year was an extremely progressive literary journal called *Angry Penguins*, published in Adelaide. One day its two editors, Max Harris and John Reed, received at their office a remarkable cultural scoop. It came in the form of a package from one Ethel Malley and contained a mass of avant-garde poetry written by her brother Ern before his death in obscure poverty at the age of 25.

Harris and Reed were so impressed with their new find that they published a special edition of their journal 'to commemorate the Australian poet Ern Malley'. When the journal was issued, two young Sydney poets laughed themselves hoarse. For they were the real authors of the 'poems', which had been composed by stringing together meaningless words and phrases at random.

The two hoaxers planned to keep their secret for a while, to prolong exposure of the experts who were so quick to praise such gibberish. But events overtook them. For South Australian police seized copies of the journal and accused Harris, as editor of the poems, of publishing indecent matter.

In court, the detective who had impounded this volume of nonsense interpreted one of the poems as being about a man who went around at night with a torch. 'I think there is a suggestion of indecency about this poem,' he said. 'I have found that people who go around parks at night do so for immoral purposes. In fact, the whole thing is indecent.'

Of another poem the detective said: 'The word incestuous is used. I don't know what it means but I regard it as being indecent.'

Harris was convicted and the detective was commended for his 'zealousness and competency'.

Brotherhood of fear

Compensation of $30,000 launched the multi-billion-dollar Mafia

No one knows for certain where the word comes from. It may be derived from a Sicilian dialect term for boldness, bluster, swank or swagger, or from the Arabic 'mehia', which means boastful. But wherever it originated, the word Mafia now means only one thing: fear.

The Mafia is the largest, most successful criminal organisation in the world. And it spells fear not only for its victims and its unwilling customers, but also for its members.

The autocratic society of the Mafia began as a resistance movement in 13th-century Sicily. It flourished over the centuries as a secret brotherhood which protected Sicilians against a succession of invaders. To the foreigners' despotism the islanders preferred even the Mafia's perverted system of justice.

By the 1940s the Mafia was so powerful that it could 'fix' the Italian Army and hand over the whole of Western Sicily to the Allies without a shot being fired.

But it is in the USA that the Mafia's grip is now the most frightening, powerful and insidious. And its reign of terror in that country dates back to two sad but well-meant blunders made by U.S. governments half a century apart.

The first was made in New Orleans in 1890 when 11 immigrant Mafiosi were lynched. Naively, the U.S. government paid $30,000 compensation to the widows of the hanged men. But the money was seized by the criminal brotherhood to launch their first organised operation of extortion.

The second blunder was Prohibition in the 1920s. In unison, the fragmented Mafia families leaped at the opportunity of supplying bootleg liquor to help 'dry' America drown its sorrows during the Depression. By the time the law was repealed in 1933, the Mafia had branched out into other criminal activities like vice, gambling and 'protection'. And when there was no longer a market in illicit liquor, the brotherhood put their amassed fortunes into seemingly respectable businesses.

The Mafia families rule by fear – often fear of each other. The gang warfare of the 1930s alerted Americans to the size of the problem in their midst. The biggest gang killing was in September 1931 when Salvatore Maranzano, head of the senior Mafia family, was murdered along with 40 of his men. But such killings also alerted the Mafiosi themselves to the dangers of advertising their power in blood.

Leaders of Mafia groups from the Atlantic to the Pacific got together to form 'The Commission', a loose-knit group of about a dozen members who respresent the nation's 24 Mafia 'families'. Always at their head is 'Il Capo di Tutti Capi', the Boss of Bosses, whose job it is to keep the younger and more fiery members in line.

The role of Il Capo di Tutti Capi was glamorised in the book and film *The Godfather*, which used as their inspiration for the title role the story of a frail old man, Carlo Gambino. Under Gambino's severe but diplomatic guidance,

---

Police at Southend, Essex, raced for their patrol cars after a woman phoned their station to report that she had seen a saloon car driving by with a body protruding from the boot.

The police eventually caught up with and flagged down the car, which had two legs sticking out of its boot.

Their owner turned out to be a helpful garage mechanic who was trying to trace a rattle for the car's driver.

WE DISPENSE WITH ACCURACY.
            – sign in London chemist's shop window

---

the Mafia flourished. He frowned on public killings, and he excluded from the families hot-headed young bloods. During his reign, there were few ritual oaths: scraps of paper burning in a new member's hand while he recites, 'This is the way I will burn if I betray the secrets of this family.'

In 1976 Carlo Gambino died peacefully in his bed at the age of 73 – and new and less respected members of the fraternity fought to become his successor. Fifty new members were immediately invited to take the oath of allegiance. And the killings began again, although more quietly and never on the scale of the 1930s gang wars.

U.S. police and government agencies have sought consolation from the Mafia's low-key approach of recent years, and they have noted with satisfaction the following facts. More than 800 members were jailed during the 1970s. In Chicago, warring families almost wiped each other out – 22 died between 1974 and 1978. In New York, the Mafia lost control of vast areas of crime, and throughout the States, its grip seemed to be slackening.

But this victory is largely illusory. The brotherhood is still so powerful that the bill for keeping Mafiosi hit-men away from the 2,000 'squealers' prepared to give evidence to the government is a staggering $20 million a year.

Moreover, the Mafia can accept the loss of a few dozen members a year to the police and FBI, since it has 3,000–5,000 criminals working for it across the country. And it can write off the loss of some of its vice and drug activities because it owns as many as 10,000 legitimate firms, producing profits estimated at $12 billion a year. That fantastic sum is five times the profits of America's largest industrial corporation, Exxon.

In the United States today, people may start their lives wrapped in a Mafia-produced nappy, listen to rock music from a Mafia record company, dine out on a Mafia steak, drive a car bought from a Mafia dealer, holiday at a Mafia hotel, buy a house on a Mafia-financed development and be buried by a Mafia funeral parlour.

Even the $12 billion a year raised from these activities is small-fry compared to the brotherhood's profits from crime. In an exhaustive survey, *Time* magazine reckoned that the Mafia takes in at least $48 billion, of which $25 billion is untaxed profit; and that, because of the mob's grip on the market, the average citizen has to pay an extra two per cent for almost everything he buys.

That is the price of a problem which a naive government tried to buy off for $30,000 in 1890.

The great pretender who duped a city's mayor

Few rogues in history have won the same fame and affection as Wilhelm Voigt. But then few have managed so successfully to poke fun at arrogance and pomposity.

It is Germany 1906. The Kaiser, his army and government officials are all-powerful, and too many soldiers and bureaucrats are too full of their own importance.

Voigt, a cobbler by trade, but a man who has spent almost half of his 57 years in jail, is free again after serving 15 years for robbery. The authorities have taken away his passport and identity card, and, in an authoritarian state, there is not much you can do without them.

But he is not one to buckle down to the system. He ponders an audacious idea. But because of the Prussian awe of authority, it is one that just might work.

Voigt buys a second-hand army uniform in a Berlin shop, and instantly turns himself into a captain in the service of the Kaiser. Next item on the agenda is some soldiers to command. Standing outside a barracks, he watches a corporal marching along with a squad of five privates.

'Corporal, where are you taking those men?' barks Voigt.

'Back to barracks, sir,' says the corporal.

'Turn them round and follow me,' snaps Voigt. 'I have an urgent mission for them on direct orders of the Kaiser himself.'

Voigt leads his little army back up the road. On the way, he orders four more soldiers to fall in and follow him. With nine men to back him, he is now a force to be reckoned with. So commandeering a bus is an easy task.

Their destination is Kopenick, an outlying district of Berlin. Once there, Voigt lines his troops up for inspection, then marches them off to the town hall. There, they burst through the door of the mayor's parlour, and confront the startled civic leader. 'You're under arrest,' snarls Voigt.

One of eight bell-ringers involved in a marathon peal at a church in Buckinghamshire, England, lost his trousers. The 56-year-old man asked if he could stop pulling on his rope to pull his trousers up. But he was told he must continue ringing for another 5,040 chimes.

'Where is your warrant?' whimpers the mayor. 'My warrant is the men I command,' roars the imperious 'captain'.

The mayor is himself a reserve officer, so he is not going to argue with orders, even if the captain's badge is on upside down, and the captain looks a little old.

Dispatching some of his men to collect the mayor's wife, Voigt turns his attention to the borough treasurer's office. There, he arrests the custodian of the town's cash, and announces: 'I am ordered to confiscate all your funds.' Meekly, the treasurer unlocks his safe and hands over 4,000 marks, worth about £650. Voigt signs a bogus receipt.

Ordering his men to hold the prisoners outside, Voigt now ransacks the office looking for a passport and identity card. But he is out of luck.

Still, he does have 4,000 marks. And he has succeeded in making a mayor, a treasurer and the army look pretty foolish. Well content with his day's work, Voigt scurries away to the railway station.

In the station's left-luggage office is a bundle of civilian clothes he took the precaution of leaving before the escapade began. Voigt heads for the lavatory. Moments later, he is in his own clothes, the uniform neatly parcelled under his arm, and on a train back to Berlin.

Next day, the newspapers are full of the exploits of the mystery man who took authority down a peg or two. Voigt is delighted. But as the days pass, and still no culprit has been arrested, he begins to feel cheated of the recognition he has earned. So he plants a photograph to help police find their way to him. And after ten days, the officers arrive to arrest him at his breakfast.

The trial is a sensation. Voigt, the man who pricked the pomposity of both army and government, is almost a national hero. And there are rumblings of discontent when the judge hands out a four-year sentence. It seems harsh.

Voigt was not to serve the full term. The Kaiser, who was said to have muttered 'amiable scoundrel' when told of his exploits, gave way to public sympathy and affection by pardoning him after 20 months.

Voigt retired in comfort to Luxembourg – on a life pension given to him by a rich Berlin dowager, who was captivated by the sheer audacity of his deeds. He died in 1922.

Joseph Samuels, convicted of killing a man in cold blood, was sent to the gallows in Sydney, Australia, in 1803. But as the trap-door opened and Samuels took 'the drop', the hangman's rope snapped and the killer survived. The hangman tried a second time, but on this occasion the trap-door only half-opened. At the third attempt, the rope broke yet again. Samuels was reprieved.

How Black Bart's one-man gang kept Wells Fargo on the run

Astagecoach robber of the Wild West who stood apart was Black Bart. He was always courteous, never hurt anybody and stole only from the treasure box and mailbags – never from the passengers.

Bart's first hold-up was on a blazing hot day in 1875 when he stopped a Wells Fargo stagecoach near Sonora, California. As the horses struggled up a hill, a strange gunman jumped out from the bushes. He wore a flour sack on his head, with holes cut out for the eyes, and a long, white coat.

He told the driver to throw down the box and mailbags, and he ordered his supposedly hidden accomplices to shoot if anyone offered resistance. The driver saw six guns poking out from the bushes. They were all trained on the stagecoach.

What followed on that day has passed into Western folklore. For when a petrified woman passenger threw her purse at Bart's feet, he calmly picked it up. With a gracious bow, he returned the purse and said he was interested only in the treasure box and mailbags, not passengers' money or valuables. This strange robber took his loot and told the driver to continue his journey.

For several years, Black Bart robbed in his cavalier manner. His reputation and courteous ways became the talk of California. And he never earned more than £250 from each of his stagecoach robberies, since most gold and valuables were by then transported by train.

The man given the task of nailing Black Bart was Jim Hume, Wells Fargo's chief detective. He soon realised that Bart was a cunning and resourceful robber. When Hume visited the scene of that first robbery, Bart's 'gang' was still there – six sticks poking through the bushes.

Hume learned little about Bart. He left no clues, his trail just petered out and he seemed to walk everywhere rather than ride. Bart became bolder and even left Hume his name and a poem at the scene of one of his hold-ups. But then he began to slip up. . . .

After a series of hold-ups, Hume visited houses in the area and learned that a grey-haired hitch-hiking stranger with a grey beard, white moustache and two missing front teeth had stopped to have dinner. A picture of the hooded raider was at last emerging.

It was a laundry mark on a handkerchief that finally led to Black Bart's capture in 1882. The thief had managed to escape unharmed when he had been interrupted by a young gunman as he was about to rob a coach, but he had blundered by leaving behind his sleeping-roll and handkerchief.

Hume had no trouble tracing the laundry mark to a San Francisco laundry – and that led him to a Mr. Bolton. He was an elderly man, softly spoken, with grey hair, grey beard, white moustache and two missing front teeth.

Mr. Bolton explained his frequent absences from home by saying that he had to make visits to his mine. But there was no mine, and Hume knew that he had his man when Black Bart's clothes were found at Mr. Bolton's home.

Black Bart was arrested and, courteous to the end, he returned much of the money taken on his raids. For their part, Wells Fargo made charges on only one hold-up and forgot about the others.

By now, the gentlemanly thief had become a popular hero. The judge must have had a soft spot for him, too. Black Bart was jailed for only six years.

The mud man who lost everything

When the Mud Man discovered 'civilisation', he also discovered crime and duplicity. The Mud Man was the name given by New Yorkers to New Guinea envoy Atairo Kanasuwo, who visited the city in 1978.

Atairo was chosen by his countrymen to represent them in New York because of his high standing in the community, as evidenced by his three wives and 25 pigs. Day after day, his body smeared with mud, he would astound New Yorkers with his elaborate tribal dances performed at the American Museum of Natural History.

One evening Atairo, tired from a hard day at the museum, was relaxing on his bunk at a city hostel when a kindly looking lady came in, gave him $5 and asked him to get some sandwiches. When he returned, the lady had disappeared – and so had all his possessions and irreplaceable tribal relics.

The Mud Man, in whose village theft is unknown, was left with only one memento of his visit to the city – an 'I love New York' badge.

BARGAIN BASEMENT UPSTAIRS.
– London store advert

Psst! Want to buy the Eiffel Tower?

Con-man sold Paris's most famous landmark - twice

If there is indeed a fool born every minute, for every fool there seems to be a con-man ready to make him a little wiser.

Two of the most extraordinary confidence tricksters of all time were Count Victor Lustig, an Austrian who worked in the French Ministry of Works, and Daniel Collins, a small-time American crook. Together they managed to sell the Eiffel Tower – not once, but twice.

The count set about pulling off the deal by booking a suite in a Paris hotel in the spring of 1925 and inviting five businessmen to meet him there. When they arrived he made them take vows of secrecy, then told them that the Eiffel Tower was in a dangerous condition and would have to be pulled down. He asked for tenders for the scrap metal contained in the famous landmark. The count explained the hotel meeting and the secrecy vow by saying that his ministry wanted to avoid any public outcry over the demolition of such a well-loved national monument.

Within the week, all bids were in and the count accepted that of scrap merchant André Poisson. The deal was struck, and a banker's draft was handed over at a final meeting at which the count introduced his 'secretary', Collins.

Then the con-men played their master-stroke. They asked Poisson for a bribe to help the deal go smoothly through official channels. The duped dealer agreed willingly, and gave the back-hander in cash. If he had ever had any suspicions, they were now wholly allayed. After all, a demand for a bribe meant that the two men must be from the ministry.

Lustig and Collins were out of the country within 24 hours. But they stayed abroad only long enough to realise that the outcry they had expected to follow their fraud had not happened. Poisson was so ashamed at being taken for a ride that he never reported the hoax to the police.

The count and his partner returned to Paris and repeated the trick. They sold the Eiffel Tower all over again to another gullible scrap merchant. This time the man did go to the police, and the con-men fled. They were never brought to justice, and they never revealed just how much money they had got away with.

Lustig's exploits may well have been inspired by a Scot, Arthur Furguson. Within a couple of months, in 1923, he sold three London landmarks to different American tourists. Buckingham Palace went for £2,000 deposit, Big Ben for £1,000 and Nelson's Column for £6,000.

He emigrated to the United States in 1925. In Washington, he found a Texas cattleman admiring the White House and, pretending to be a government agent, spun a slender yarn about how the administration was looking for

ways of cutting costs. Now, if the Texan would care to rent the White House at a knockdown rate of $100,000 a year . . .? Furguson was in business again.

The Scotsman moved to New York where he explained to an Australian visitor that, because of a widening scheme for New York Harbour, the Statue of Liberty would have to be dismantled and sold. A great loss to the USA, but would it not look grand in Sydney Harbour . . .?

The Australian immediately began to raise the $100,000 that the con-man asked for the statue. But his bankers advised him to make a few further inquiries, and the police were tipped off.

Furguson was arrested, and a court sentenced him to five years in jail. When he came out, the master-hoaxer retired from the ancient-monuments business and, until his death in 1938, he lived in California – languishing in luxury on his ill-gotten gains.

All that glittered was not gold

Greed over-rode commercial commonsense among the backers who queued to pour cash into the pockets of two German tricksters – Franz Tausend and Heinrich Kurschaldgen. For the pair claimed that they could manufacture gold.

Tausend and Kurschalden never worked together, but they both used similar methods to prise cash out of the wallets of the gullible.

Tausend was a former travelling tinker who had briefly studied chemistry in Zurich. His claim that he could make gold by mixing lead and solder was so convincing that level-headed businessmen and even aristocrats contributed to his Chemical Research Society.

One of the original backers was influential Rhineland industrialist Alfred Mannesmann, who paid £5,000 into the society. Another was Erich Ludendorff, the famous World War One general, who saw Tausend's discovery as a way of easing Germany's war debts.

For a short time, Tausend paid dividends on investors' cash so that none of them would realise they were being led up the garden path. But then the double-talking tinker became greedy. With the £125,000 he had collected, he bought two magnificent castles near Bolzano, Italy, and fitted them out

with the best that money could buy. His ex-waitress wife even assumed the title of baroness.

Reports of the lavish hospitality offered at the castles made investors suspicious and they began to investigate. They had Tausend arrested and brought back to Germany. In 1931, he was convicted of fraud and jailed for three years and eight months.

While Tausend was living in style in Italy, Kurschaldgen was also enjoying the good life by claiming that he could make gold and even radium. Kurschaldgen, who had not studied chemistry since his schooldays, relied on his eloquence and impressive laboratory equipment to dupe the wealthy of north-west Germany and beyond into financing his work.

He had a simple method of convincing hard-headed businessmen that he could manufacture gold. In demonstrations at his laboratory, investors saw him mix flasks of sand and water. The mixture was turned into gold by an electric current. Only later was it discovered that tiny grains of gold had secretly been added to the water.

Kurschaldgen was reputed to have made about £10,000 from his regular investors. A British consortium was hoodwinked into paying him £50 a month, and an American millionaire offered him £50,000 for the secret of his discovery.

But, like Tausend, Kurschaldgen became greedy. He began to live the high life – and to give the game away. He was brought before a court at Dusseldorf in 1930 and jailed for 18 months.

Chapter
Four

Victors
and Vanquished

The Japanese attacked Pearl Harbor and found the defenders sadly unprepared. The U.S. 7th Cavalry attacked Sitting Bull's camp at Little Bighorn and found the defenders surprisingly well prepared. The story of war is full of mistakes – mistakes that have cost dearly in wasted lives.

The rise and fall of General Custer

Vanity led him to death in the ill-fated 'Last Stand'

General George Armstrong Custer was known by the Indians as Pahuskà, the 'Long-Haired One', because of the flowing straw-coloured locks of which he was so proud. He was also known as 'Hard Backsides' because of the long chases he made without leaving the saddle. But he was best known to the Indians of the North American Plains as a callous mass-killer – an annihilator of entire tribes.

Custer, who was in command of the famous U.S. 7th Cavalry, gained his bloody reputation when, in 1868, he was sent by General Philip Sheridan, the 'Angry Bear' of the frontier forts, to subjugate the Plains Indians who refused to be herded into the reservations set by for them. Why Custer should have been picked for this important task is a matter for conjecture. For his career as a soldier had been extremely patchy.

He was born on December 5, 1839, in New Rumley, Ohio. He graduated from the U.S. Military Academy, West Point, and, thanks to the Civil War – in which he distinguished himself by his pursuit of the Confederate Commander-in-Chief, General Robert E. Lee – he soared to the rank of brigadier-general at the age of only 23.

Success went to Custer's head. He became a vain, flamboyant glory-seeker. He grew his blond hair shoulder-length and covered the walls of his room with pictures of himself. When the Civil War ended in 1865, Brigadier-General Custer's ego was severely deflated when he was returned to the rank of captain. He became something of a laughing stock among his men, but within a year had fought his way back to the rank of lieutenant-colonel.

It was then that his self-esteem almost became his undoing. Without consulting senior officers, he decided to take a vacation – and left his camp to visit his wife, Libbie. Custer was court-martialled and suspended for a year without pay. He used the time to write about his own adventures in the most heroic terms. He also ran up bills which, as he later moved from fort to fort, never quite seemed to catch up with him.

In 1868 he was reinstated and given a special mission – one that required tact, diplomacy and compassion. Newly promoted General George Armstrong Custer, aged 28, had none of these virtues, yet he was sent off to solve once and for all the problems of the Plains Indians.

The Indians, mainly Cheyennes and Sioux, had been slowly pushed westwards by land-hungry white men for decades. But in the 1860s, the process was speeded up. This was because roaming bands of Indian buffalo hunters were becoming an embarrassment to the authorities – despite the fact that land treaties had allowed the Indians this freedom of movement. Now the authorities wanted the land on which the buffalo roamed. It was decided that those Indians who had not so far settled down in reservations to subsist on meagre government handouts must at last be made to toe the line.

Custer was reckoned to be just the man to get the message across.

In the autumn of 1868, a peaceable old chief called Black Kettle, leader of the Southern Cheyennes, settled down with his tribe for the winter on the bank of the Washita River, about 100 miles from the nearest white military outpost, Fort Cobb. He asked that the 200 families within his branch of the tribe be allowed to move to the protection of the fort for the winter, but he was refused. General William Hazen, the fort's commander, told Black Kettle and his deputation to return to the Washita, where they would be allowed to remain until after the snows had melted.

> **President Lincoln said of General Ambrose Burnside:**
> **'Only he could wring spectacular defeat out of the jaws of**
> **victory.' At the Battle of Antietam, during the American**
> **Civil War in 1862, Burnside ordered his troops to advance**
> **across a narrow bridge over a river. They could hardly**
> **cross more than two abreast, and were mown down by**
> **Confederate gunners. What Burnside had not considered**
> **was that the river was less than three feet deep and his**
> **army could have walked across unhindered.**

THE WORLD'S GREATEST MISTAKES

The assurance meant nothing. For, in December 1868, Custer was sent in to make an example of Black Kettle's people. Before dawn one foggy morning, Pahuska, the Long-Haired One, ordered his men to surround the Cheyenne camp. When the soldiers appeared through the mist, Black Kettle had his horse saddled and set out alone to parley with them. He did not know that Custer's mission was 'to proceed to Washita River, the winter seat of the hostile tribes, and there to destroy their villages and ponies, kill or hang all warriors and bring back all women and children'.

Black Kettle had hardly left the perimeter of the camp on his mission of peace when the cavalry charged. According to Indian legend, he was shot dead as he raised his hand to halt the approaching soldiers. Custer organised the massacre that followed. His orders were to kill the warriors, but the executions were indiscriminate. More than 100 Cheyennes were shot dead, only about a tenth of them warriors. The rest were women, children and old men. Hundreds of ponies were also slaughtered so that the survivors would have no means of flight. And 50 women and children were taken prisoner.

Fear and hatred of Custer spread among the tribes and was nurtured over the following months as he launched pitiless campaigns against all other Indians in the area.

This then was Custer, the man chosen by Washington to make the West safe for civilised Christians, the man who by treachery and butchery forced the surrender of one tribal chief after another – until he met his match in Sitting Bull.

Tatanka Yotanka, or Sitting Bull, was a leader of the Hunkpapa, the fiercest and most independent branch of the Sioux nation. Sioux means Dakota, and it was there and in neighbouring Montana that Custer discovered he was not invincible.

In 1868, the Black Hills of Dakota had been given for all time to the Indians who lived there. Many tribes considered the hills, the 'Paha Sapa', to be holy places and the centre of the spirit world. The treaty suited the white man in 1868 because he considered them valueless. But it did not suit him six years later when Custer led an expedition into the hills and reported: 'They are full of gold from the grass roots down.' The treaty was immediately disregarded and Custer pushed a trail through to open up the wealth of the Black Hills. The Indians called it the 'Thieves' Road'.

A commission was sent out from Washington to negotiate with the Sioux, Arapahos and Cheyennes who had claims to the Black Hills. But the tribes were not willing to sell their holy ground or to swop it for other territory. Sitting Bull told the commissioners: 'We want to sell none of our land – not even a pinch of dust. The Black Hills belong to us. We want no white men here. If the white man tries to take the hills, we will fight.'

Unable to get the precious Black Hills by fair means, the white man tried foul. The war department issued an ultimatum that any Indians not on their official reservations by the end of January 1876 would be considered hostile and that 'military force will be sent to compel them'. Sitting Bull received news of the ultimatum only three weeks before the deadline and he protested that his tribe could not contemplate moving camp in mid-winter. On February 7 General Sheridan – the man who had once announced that 'the only good Indian is a dead one' – was ordered to attack. And the man he chose to deal the major blow against his most formidable enemy, Sitting Bull, was his faithful executioner, Custer.

Throughout the early months of 1876, roving troops of horse soldiers drove tribes of peaceful Indians out of the Powder River and Tongue River Basins near the Montana-Wyoming border. With their tepees burned, their horses killed and with little warm clothing, the straggling groups of survivors, led by Sitting Bull, gathered in a ragged but proud band in the 'Valley Of The Greasy Grass' – the Little Bighorn valley.

As the army's aims became increasingly obvious, every Indian who was not part of the Little Bighorn camp felt isolated and threatened. Members of tribes who would previously have chosen to remain well apart joined Sitting Bull's settlement. Even Indians who had long since resigned themselves to life on the reservations deserted them in their thousands to flock to the Little Bighorn valley.

According to a white scout, Lewis Dewitt: 'Sitting Bull had a great power over the Sioux. He knew how to lead them. He told the Sioux many times that he was not made to be a reservation Indian. The Great Spirit had made him free to go wherever he wished, to hunt buffalo and to be a leader of his tribe.'

By June of 1876, there were gathered together in the valley Sitting Bull's Hunkpapas, the Oglalas of his ally Crazy Horse, Blackfoot Sioux, Arapahos, Sans Arcs, Brules, Minneconjous and Cheyennes – in a forest of tepees and makeshift tents stretching three miles along the west bank of the Little Bighorn River. There were at least 10,000 Indians, of whom some 3,000 or 4,000 were warriors.

Mrs. Mary Wilson was entertaining friends at No. 10 Downing Street while her husband, Harold, then prime minister, was working upstairs. The discussion turned to theology and one of the guests said: 'Fortunately, there is the one above who knows all the answers.'

'Yes,' replied Mrs. Wilson, not realising the significance of the remark, 'Harold will be down in a few moments.'

THE WORLD'S GREATEST MISTAKES

They all knew that the big battle was coming. It would be the last chance for the Sioux to hold on to the land of their ancestors and their gods. So they held a sun dance.

The dance was the greatest celebration the Sioux nation had ever known. The spring grass was by now lush and the buffalo plentiful, so they filled their bellies, danced and tested their courage. Sitting Bull, his body already marked with the numerous scars of previous sun dances, had 50 pieces of flesh cut from each arm for this occasion. He then danced non-stop around the sacred pole, staring constantly at the sun. When dusk fell, he continued dancing – through the night and into the next day. After 18 hours, he fainted. When he was revived, he told the tribe that he had seen a wonderful vision. He had seen white soldiers 'falling like grasshoppers' into his camp while a voice said: 'I give you these because they have no ears.'

Victory was assured!

Custer also had visions – of his own glory. At the time of the Sioux sun dance, he was heading towards the Little Bighorn from Fort Abraham Lincoln, far to the east in North Dakota. Every night in camp, he would sit and write self-congratulatory dispatches to a New York newspaper. He also committed his 'private' thoughts to his diary – with, of course, a view to having them published later for posterity.

He wrote: 'In years long-numbered with the past, my every thought was ambitious. Not to be wealthy, not to be learned, but to be great. I desired to link my name with acts and men, and in such a manner as to be a mark of honour, not only to the present, but to future generations.'

This then was the man who arrived at the valley of the Little Bighorn, across the river from Sitting Bull's camp, on the night of June 24, 1876. Custer had with him just 611 men, 12 troops of the U.S. Cavalry – only a small part of the offensive force. But, in true Custer style, he had outstripped all other units and was far ahead of the field, ready for battle.

Straggling far to the south was General George Crook, leading 1,000 soldiers and 250 Sioux-hating Crows and Shoshonis from Fort Fetterman. They had been delayed – and all but defeated – in an ambush by Crazy Horse's Oglalas, who had made a daring sortie from their camp to halt the white men in the valley of the River Rosebud. In fact, under Crook's haphazard generalship, his force would have been obliterated but for the bravery of his Indian allies. As it was, his column was in disarray and had no chance of meeting up with the other forces descending on the Little Bighorn.

Custer knew none of this. He did know, however, that he was well ahead of the other two leaders who were also vying for the glory of wiping out the Indian 'hostiles'. They were Major-General John Gibbon, who had marched east from Fort Ellis, and General Alfred Terry, who had marched west from

Sitting Bull.

Retired tailor Harold Senby had been wearing a hearing
aid for 20 years but it never seemed to have done him much
good. Harold, aged 74, discovered the reason why when he
went to Leeds Hospital for a routine check-up . . . and was
told that he had been wearing it in the wrong ear. Harold
said: 'It appears there was a mix-up when it was first fitted.
The aid was moulded to fit my left ear instead of my right
one. I always thought it was pretty useless.'

Fort Abraham Lincoln to meet up with Gibbon on the Yellowstone River.
The two were now moving up the Little Bighorn with a combined force of
1,500 men.

Terry was Custer's superior, and the two generals should have been riding
together. But Terry, lacking experience in Indian fighting, had given in to
Custer's pleadings to be allowed to advance and reconnoitre the Sioux camp.
Fearful that anyone else might reach the camp before him, Custer turned
down Terry's offer of extra men and Gatling guns and raced ahead, boasting:
'I could whip all the Indians on the continent with the 7th Cavalry.'

Custer's confidence had never once deserted him. He had driven his 12
troops of men mercilessly – they had made 60 miles in just two days – and he
was unperturbed even when he discovered the true size of the force he was
seeking to take on in battle. The first clue to the strength of the Sioux came
when Custer's men encountered the tracks that the Indians had left when they
had moved their camp sites a few days earlier. The tracks, beaten up by the
hoofs of their ponies and the dragging of their tepee poles, were more than a
mile wide.

The second clue came from Custer's own Indian scouts. They begged their
leader to hold back for two days until Terry and Gibbon were due to arrive.
But Pahuska, the arrogant glory-seeker, could not wait – and his vanity was
his undoing.

Custer's plan was to split up his 12 troops into three battalions, which would
launch simultaneous attacks on the Indians' camp from different directions. So
at first light on June 25, he gave three troops to Captain Frederick Benteen and
three to Major Marcus Reno, took five himself, and left the remaining one
with the supply train.

Sitting Bull's scouts kept a careful watch on the slow progress of Custer and
his main force of 225 men, who were moving down the river valley but hidden
from the river itself by a long bluff. Custer was looking for a suitable crossing
place for a surprise attack on the village – but the Indians knew that he would
not find one.

At the other end of the camp, the Indians were less vigilant. While their attention was focused on the main cavalry force, Major Reno's modest battalion of 140 men crossed the river and attacked on schedule from the rear – taking the Indians largely by surprise. As he led his charge, Reno confidently expected Custer to be attacking the other side of the village at the same time. He had no way of knowing that Custer's battalion was still stumbling down the valley some four miles away.

Reno surprised the Oglalas, Hunkpapas and Blackfoot Sioux in their villages at the southern end of the great encampment. Women and children fled from their tepees under a hail of bullets. A young Hunkpapa named Gall, an orphan who had been adopted by Sitting Bull as his chief lieutenant, saw his wife and children cut down before he was able to rally his warriors for a counter-attack.

Gall led his men around Reno's flank and, when the cavalry momentarily faltered and failed to press their charge, he caught them from behind. Out-flanked and outnumbered, Reno's soldiers, by now exhausted from their forced march, retreated to the comparative safety of nearby woodland to shelter until Custer's attack had drawn off the full fury of the Indians.

But Custer had still not attacked. Nor had the third column, under Captain Benteen, who was still some miles from his target. After only 30 minutes of battle, Major Reno's withdrawal was turned into a total rout. The Indians could now concentrate their full attention on the hated Pahuska. . . .

Sitting Bull stood in front of his tepee and directed the battle through a continuous stream of pony messengers. Gall, Crazy Horse and Cheyenne leader Two Moons galloped the three-mile length of the encampment, rallying the warriors to the battle about to commence.

Crazy Horse cried: 'Hoka-hey! It's a good day to fight. It's a good day to die. Strong hearts, brave hearts to the front . . . weak hearts and cowards to the rear.'

Custer's column was still hidden from Sitting Bull's camp by the hills. The general was advancing carefully but confidently, seeking the ideal break in the bluff through which to charge the Indian villages across the river. But unknown to him, the river had already been forded – by Gall's men. They swept through a ravine and hit the rear of the cavalry column. Custer was

---

When ad-men for Pepsi-Cola had their slogan 'Come alive with Pepsi' translated into Mandarin Chinese, the translation turned out to mean: 'Pepsi brings your ancestors back from the grave.'

---

taken completely by surprise. He ordered his men to race for a nearby hill and take up defensive positions. But when still only half way up the rise, the general saw a sight that must have made him realise for the first time that he was not invincible.

There, on the top of the rise that is now called Custer's Hill, appeared Crazy Horse – and 1,000 mounted warriors. For a moment, they peered down disdainfully at Custer and his straggling band of exhausted cavalry. Then, whooping and shouting and screaming, they charged down the hill.

The cavalry were surrounded within seconds. The soldiers dismounted and set about defending themselves on open ground with hardly a hint of cover. They fought bravely, trying to hold on to their horses. But as the shrieking Sioux closed in, the cavalry had to let their mounts go. There was now no hope of escape. The proud cavalrymen were reduced to a handful. On the edges of the battle, a few wounded soldiers held up their arms and asked to be taken prisoner. But there were no prisoners taken that day. The wounded were shot or hacked to death.

Custer was one of the last to die. As his ranks thinned and the Indians got nearer to him, they saw that Pahuska no longer had shoulder-length hair. He

had had it cut, which was why the attackers had failed to recognise him instantly.

The general stood at the centre of a pathetically small group of survivors. Sitting Bull said: 'Where the last stand was made, the Long-Haired One stood like a sheaf of corn with all the ears fallen around him.' Then Custer was covered by a wave of Indian warriors.

Many Indians claimed later to have been the one who had killed the hated Pahuska. It was a proud boast. In Washington, however, Custer's Last Stand was labelled a savage massacre. A stronger force was sent against the Indians, who quickly scattered.

Crazy Horse moved to a reservation and surrendered. But he was arrested and bayonetted to death while trying to escape from Fort Robinson in 1877. His last words were: 'Let me go, my friends. You have got me hurt enough.'

Sitting Bull fled with 3,000 warriors to Canada, the 'Land of the Great Godmother', Queen Victoria. He returned to the U.S. and surrendered in 1881. He spent two years in prison before being allowed to rejoin his tribe at Standing Rock reservation, North Dakota. He was the star of Buffalo Bill Cody's Wild West Show for a while but, after returning to his tribe once again, he was accused by the army of inciting unrest. When Indian police arrived to take him to jail on December 15, 1890, Sitting Bull resisted arrest and was shot in the back.

The vanquished Custer, on the other hand, received greater honours than the persecuted victors. His body was recovered and given a hero's burial at West Point. Even the lone survivor of the bloodbath – a cavalry horse ironically named Comanche – was honoured as the 7th Cavalry's mascot, always appearing on parades saddled but riderless.

Custer left for posterity a self-congratulatory book, *My Life On The Plains*, a phoney legend of heroism that it took a century to dispel. There is also devoted to his memory a small but thriving business at the Little Bighorn. It sells bottles of 'The Dust That Custer Bit'.

The Oxford University dons who turned up for a lecture by the eminent psychologist Dr. Emil Busch were puzzled but impressed. The man they had come to see after answering an advertisement in an Oxford newspaper had a flowing beard, a strong German accent and a strange way of haranguing his audience so that most of what he said was unintelligible. They learned later that 'Dr. Busch' was one of their undergraduates and that his entire speech had been gibberish.

Left. General Percival on his way to surrender Singapore to General Yamashita.

The fall of Singapore

How the Japanese took the 'Bastion of the British Empire' by bluff

Black rain fell on Singapore on Sunday, February 15, 1942. It fell through clouds of smoke billowing from the blazing oil storage tanks that the British had ordered to be burnt so that they would not fall into the hands of the invading Japanese. The British would not be needing the oil any more. They were surrendering.

The capitulation of the 'impregnable' natural fortress island of Singapore was the end of a long invasion road for the Japanese. But it was the end of an even longer road for the British. For when the Allied troops – outwitted, outfought and outmanoeuvred – handed over Singapore to the Japanese, they were also handing over imperial control in Asia. Above all, they were presaging the end of the British Empire – the destruction of the myth that Britain could protect her far-flung colonies from all comers.

And it need not have been so. When the Japanese invasion forces landed and began their long sweep down the Malay Peninsula, they were heavily outnumbered by the British, Australian and Indian forces who stood in their path. The Japanese, commanded by General Tomoyuki Yamashita, started out with no airfields, no naval cover and an inferior armoury. They made up for it with determination, imagination and brutality.

The Japanese overcame resistance by going around it. Whenever the Allies drew up new defence lines, the Japanese took to the sea in stolen boats and landed further down the coast. The Royal Navy was nowhere to be seen. The promised ships for the defence of Malaya and Singapore, Britain's primary naval base in the Far East, never arrived. Nor did the promised air reinforcements. There was nothing to stop the Japanese.

For most of their journey south towards Singapore, the enemy were able to pedal on bicycles along tracks through what was thought to be impenetrable jungle, guided by no more than school atlases. At the beginning of February 1942 they arrived, along with their captured planes, guns and trucks, at Johore, at the foot of the Malay Peninsula, and looked across the narrow Johore Strait at the stronghold they were determined to win – Singapore.

Singapore is an island about 20 miles long by 10 miles wide, joined to the mainland by a 1,100-yard causeway. To the south of the island, facing out to sea, is Singapore City, peopled by Malays and Chinese. To the north, facing the mainland, was what was then thought to be one of the most important military strongpoints in the world – the Royal Navy base.

For a century, Singapore had been the cornerstone of Britain's supremacy in the Far East. It was labelled the 'Gibraltar of the East' and the 'Bastion of the British Empire'. But it was neither of these. Because of the strange military blindness that seems to have afflicted so many of Britain's wartime leaders, Singapore was fortified against an attack from the sea but was wide open to a landing across the Johore Strait.

Singapore had slumbered for too long to be in any way prepared for the barbarous, murderous, raping, looting army that was about to overwhelm it. Not until two days before Christmas of 1941 did Lieutenant-General Percival, leader of the British Malaya Command, order a survey of the north coast of the island to plan defensive works. No action was taken on his order for two weeks.

Winston Churchill was not fully alerted to the risible state of Singapore's defences until January 16, when he received a telegram about them from General Wavell, who had recently been appointed Supreme Commander of the area. Churchill immediately sent a long and urgent directive to his chiefs of staff:

Fire-fighters labouring to quench the flames created by Japanese bombers.

'I must confess to being staggered by Wavell's telegram. . . . Merely to have seaward defences and no forts or fixed defences to protect the rear is not to be excused on any ground. I warn you this will be one of the greatest scandals that could possibly be exposed.

'Let a plan be made at once to do the best possible while the battle on Johore is going forward. This plan should comprise: an attempt to use the fortress guns on the northern front by firing reduced charges; mining and obstructing possible landing places; wiring and laying booby traps in mangrove swamps and other places; placing field batteries at each end of the Strait; forming the nuclei of three or four mobile counter-attack reserve columns upon which the troops, when driven out of Johore, can be based; and employing the entire male civilian population on constructing defence works, the most rigorous compulsion being used.

'Not only must the defence of Singapore Island be maintained by every means, but the whole island must be fought for until every single unit and every single strongpoint has been separately destroyed. Finally, the city of Singapore must be converted into a citadel and defended to the death. No surrender can be contemplated.'

His exhortations came too late for the defenders of Singapore. The defence works had not been put in hand soon enough. The civilian population was in such disorder that few construction projects could be started. The labourers had fled. Even some of the British and Australian troops had deserted and fled to other islands. There was also a strong fifth-column of Japanese businessmen in Singapore City. The scene was set for a military disaster.

Wavell believed that, even after the loss of Johore, Singapore could hold out for months. By then, American reinforcements, including aircraft carriers, would be in the area. Such a delay to the Japanese advance would allow time for a spring counter-offensive to be launched from the Dutch East Indies.

Yamashita had other ideas for his Japanese 25th Army. He wanted to sweep through the Indies and invade Australia. His key targets were Sydney and Brisbane, and he foresaw no major obstacles to their capture. But first: Singapore. And Yamashita knew that Singapore would have to be taken quickly, otherwise his long-stretched supply lines would be unable to sustain the offensive. His soldiers each had only 100 rounds of ammunition.

On January 31, the last British and Australian troops crossed the long causeway from Johore to the island. They were played across by the only two surviving pipers of the Argyll and Sutherland Highlanders; more than half of the pipers' regiment had been wiped out on the long retreat south.

After the last remnants of the fleeing forces had crossed, charges were set on a bridge section of the 70-foot wide causeway, carrying a road and railway. The causeway was breached. But when the Japanese examined it at low tide, they found that the sunken structure was only four feet underwater. If they wished, they could wade across.

Yamashita set up his forward command post in the tower of the palace of the Sultan of Johore. From there he watched the Japanese Air Force, outnumbering the Royal Air Force planes ten to one, pound the British and Australians, who were desperately trying to build their inadequate defences. Yamashita's tower was never shelled because it was considered too obvious a target for an enemy to occupy. While the Japanese general watched the action first-hand, Wavell

---

An undercover marshal seeking a witness to a crime in Dallas, Texas, sidled up to a girl standing provocatively in a darkened street and began sweet-talking her. The girl slapped a pair of handcuffs on him and marched him off to jail. She too was an undercover cop.

was far away in his Java headquarters, hampered by abysmal communications. The tactics for the defence of Singapore were left in the hands of General Arthur Edward Percival.

Percival decided to stretch his forces along the northern coastline to ward off the Japanese before they could land on the island. Churchill's idea for a strike force to repulse the enemy once they had landed was not thought by Percival to be the best policy. He knew that the morale of his troops was low and that the morale of the civilian population was lower. It did not help when soldiers saw the naval base installations that they had fought for so long to protect being blown up by their own side to prevent them from falling into the hands of the Japanese.

Percival had 85,000 men on Singapore, 15,000 of them non-combatants. They faced between 30,000 and 50,000 crack Japanese troops across the Strait. In terms of firepower, the two sides were well matched. But in all other respects the Japanese held the advantage. They ruled the skies. Their morale was higher: they were elated by victory, and they relished their glorious task

British soldiers taken prisoner by the Japanese.

of 'liberating' Singapore from white colonial domination. They would carry it out with fanatical zeal.

Wavell visited Singapore on January 20 to discuss defence plans with Percival. Wavell said he thought the enemy would land off the north-west of the island. Percival disagreed. He believed the attack would come from the north-east, and he decided to put his freshest troops there. The battered Australians would defend the north-west coastline. On February 8, after days of fierce air and artillery bombardment, Wavell was proved to have been right.

At 10.30 p.m. the Japanese landed in the north-west sector, held by the Australian Brigade. The coast at that point was covered by searchlights but the troops were told to keep them switched off, so as not to give away their positions, until an order to the contrary was issued. But the artillery barrage had cut all telephone lines, and so the order was never given. The invisible enemy came ashore and formed a strong beach-head. By 3 a.m. they were four miles inland. The Australians fell back to agreed lines, but in the darkness and the confusion, many went astray. A planned counter-attack had to be cancelled.

When the news was reported to Percival, he was visibly shaken. But there was worse to come. A further string of landings was reported. Because of lack of communications, units who feared they were in danger of being encircled pulled out of their strong positions without ever coming under attack. The whole front was falling apart. Finally, enemy tanks were sighted south of the causeway and on the main road to Singapore City.

The battle seemed to have been lost within a matter of hours. But the Japanese took time to build up their supplies from across the Strait. By the evening of February 9, about 25,000 men had crossed the Johore Strait in an armada of tiny boats, rafts and rubber dinghies. Many had swum across. It was a remarkable feat – no less remarkable than the disorganised state of the defending forces. The battle-weary Australians of the 22nd and neighbouring 27th Brigades fought hard, but they were badly organised. With them were the Japanese-hating Chinese civilian defence units, who refused to fall back even when the regular soldiers were ordered to do so.

Notorious gangster John Dillinger thought he had a sure-fire way of evading arrest. U.S. federal agents had a record of his finger-prints, so Dillinger decided to acquire new ones. He dipped all his fingers and thumbs in a saucer of acid and had to endure a period of agony before they healed again. After several weeks, Dillinger tested his new fingerprints – and found that they were exactly the same as the old ones.

THE WORLD'S GREATEST MISTAKES

At one stage of the battle, the Australians prevented further Japanese landings by draining oil storage tanks into the mangrove swamps – then setting fire to them. Many of the enemy were burned alive, and the invasion of the island was delayed. The Japanese took their revenge. They beheaded 200 wounded soldiers.

Then came two major errors which sealed the fate of Singapore. Just as the Japanese Imperial Guards Division was seeking permission to abandon its positions near the causeway because of intense opposition from a battalion of the Australian 27th, the Australians pulled back. The decision has never been explained. But it left a 4,000-yard gap through which the enemy poured unimpeded. At the same time, Percival drew up contingency plans which involved falling back to reserve lines around the perimeter of Singapore City. The intention was that the plans should be studied but not acted upon. But somewhere along the line the message got garbled – and the Australian 22nd Brigade, which was bearing the brunt of the attack, pulled back to the reserve lines. The 12th Indian Brigade, finding itself isolated, also pulled back to new positions.

On that day, too, the last RAF fighter flew out of Singapore. Had the RAF remained, it was said, it would have been obliterated as Japanese dive-bombers wrecked the airfields. Unhindered, the enemy aircraft turned their entire destructive power on Singapore City, with its population doubled by refugees to one million. The closely packed buildings were swept by fire, and the streets literally ran with blood. The water supply was almost entirely cut off by bomber attacks. Bodies lay in the gutters. An epidemic was now a certainty.

On February 10, Wavell flew in from Java for the last time and ordered an immediate counter-attack. Percival resisted the order. But on Wavell's insistence, the attack went ahead – and failed miserably. It had been launched too late.

Churchill cabled Wavell: 'I think you ought to realise the way we view the situation in Singapore. Percival is reported to have over 100,000 men, and it is doubtful whether the Japanese have as many in the whole Malay peninsula. In these circumstances, the defenders must greatly outnumber the Japanese forces and in a well-contested battle they should destroy them. There must at this stage be no thought of saving the troops. The honour of the British Empire and the British Army is at stake. The whole reputation of our country and our race is involved.'

Churchill's estimate of 100,000 British troops was an extreme exaggeration, but the war leader's anger got through. Percival told his officers: 'In some units, troops have not shown the fighting spirit expected of men of the British Empire. It will be a lasting disgrace if we are defeated by an army of clever gangsters, many times inferior in numbers to our own.'

Wavell also weighed in: 'It is certain that our troops on Singapore heavily outnumber Japanese troops who have crossed the Strait. We must destroy them. Our whole fighting reputation is at stake, and the honour of the British Empire. It will be disgraceful if we yield our boasted fortress of Singapore to inferior enemy forces.'

But the exhortations were in vain. Many of the soldiers, who through the length of the Malay Peninsula had fought so valiantly, had suddenly lost the will to fight. There were disgraceful scenes as armed deserters roamed the streets, looting stores. They even fought women for places on the last small boats leaving Singapore harbour.

The Governor of Singapore, Sir Shenton Thomas, ordered all liquor in the city to be destroyed so that victorious Japanese soldiers would not go on a drunken orgy of murder and rape. Percival ordered the Military Nursing Service to be evacuated by boat so that they would not suffer the usual sordid fate of white women prisoners of the Japanese. (When the Japanese did capture a hospital on the outskirts of Singapore City, they bayonetted patients and staff.)

On February 13, Percival called a meeting with Lieutenant-General Sir Lewis Heath, of the 3rd Indian Corps, and Major-General Gordon Bennett,

General Yamashita inspecting the devastation in Singapore.

Left General Yamashita.   *Right* Lt.-General Percival, aged 76.

of the 8th Australian Division. Both said that a counter-attack would certainly fail. Both advocated capitulation.

Percival held out, hoping for a miracle – that if the Japanese ran their supplies too low they might have to ease up the barrage that was crippling the city, and that this would allow time for reinforcements to arrive by sea. But on the afternoon of February 15, the Chinese New Year's Day, he gave up hope. A Japanese plane had dropped a package near his headquarters. It was tied with red and white ribbons which streamed out behind it as it fell to the ground. Inside was a message from Yamashita. It began: 'In a spirit of chivalry, we have the honour of advising you to surrender. . . .'

Percival knew that the city had only a week's food supplies left, and only a day's water. He knew that if the fighting continued, tens of thousands of the frightened civilians besieged there would soon be dead. And he took seriously a veiled threat in Yamashita's note: 'If you continue resistance, it will be difficult to bear with patience from a humanitarian point of view.'

Under a pall of black smoke and a downpour of blackened rain, Percival drove out of the city to meet his stony-faced Japanese counterpart across a table at the island's Ford car assembly plant. There, the tall 55-year-old British general unconditionally surrendered the 'Bastion of the British Empire'.

Yamashita bowed formally – and breathed a secret sigh of relief. He later wrote in his diary: 'My attack on Singapore was a bluff. I had 30,000 men and was outnumbered more than three to one. I knew that if I had been made to fight longer for Singapore I would have been beaten. That was why the surrender had to be immediate. I was extremely frightened that the British would discover our numerical weakness and lack of supplies and force me into disastrous street fighting. But they never did. My bluff worked.'

The hills of Hell

Eight months of killing ended with neither side the victor

Sir William Birdwood.

It was the most daring strategic plan of World War One: in one move, to break the terrible stalemate in the trenches of France by opening up a new front in the east. The plan was Winston Churchill's. The First Lord of the Admiralty, as he then was, believed that by attacking Germany's ally, Turkey, he could slit 'the soft underbelly' of the Kaiser's Europe. He would do it by smashing through the Dardanelles Strait, cutting off the Turks from the Germans and linking Britain with her ally, Russia, through the Black Sea.

THE WORLD'S GREATEST MISTAKES

It was a brilliant plan whose success relied on surprising the Turks on both land and sea. It required a strong naval force to sweep through the Dardanelles, plus an amphibious force to secure the heights on either side.

But for all the scheme's brilliant conception, the execution of it was a disaster. For the Turks were well warned of the British intentions.

On November 3, 1914, Royal Navy ships sailed up the Dardanelles Strait and launched a ten-minute bombardment on the Turkish forts. That ten minutes caused little damage but gave the game away entirely. The Turks, under German military guidance, began mining the Strait and reinforcing the defences along the difficult, mountainous country of the Gallipoli peninsula. They were able to do this at their leisure, because they were not bothered again by the Allies for a further three months.

On February 19, 1915, a much larger force of British and French ships began again bombarding the Turkish forts. The Turks immediately moved out of range of the naval guns, waited patiently for the bombardment to end, then returned to their positions. The attack availed the Allies little – and lost the British and French three battleships sunk by mines and three more disabled. The First Sea Lord, Admiral Fisher, reported: 'Things are going badly at the Dardanelles. We are held up for want of soldiers.'

Back in London, many of the War Cabinet wondered whether it was worth proceeding with the plan to take the Dardanelles. Not Churchill. He never wavered, and his enthusiasm for the project carried the majority of the war leaders with him.

So, in the early hours of April 25, 1915 – five months after the first warning shots were fired – the biggest amphibious force the world had known headed for the Gallipoli beaches.

There were 1,500 Australians and New Zealanders in the first assault. They were disgorged from three battleships into small boats, and at 4 a.m. they began rowing towards the black shore. In the early dawn light they approached the cove of Ari Burnu – but instead of seeing the wide, gently sloping beach they had been led to expect, all they saw were precipitous cliffs and barren hills. From the top of those hills a flare went up and suddenly a rain of bullets poured down on the little boats. The soldiers leaped into the sea and struggled ashore, weighed down by their packs. Many failed to make the beach, but those who did fixed their bayonets and stood waiting for the mass of Turks who were now running, slipping and tumbling down the hills in front of them. The battle had begun within yards of the water's edge of what was to be known for ever after as Anzac Cove.

The Australians and New Zealanders were all volunteer soldiers who had answered the call to defend the British Empire, of which they were the furthest-flung members. They were raw and not expected to put up a sustained

> **Police opened the back of a refrigerated truck after complaints that it was parked without lights in a London street. Inside they found the nearly frozen driver, who had locked himself in three hours earlier.**

fight. But their heroism, tenacity and sheer guts at Anzac Cove became a legend. They pushed the Turks back off the shoreline and pursued them with flashing bayonets up into the hills. The grand battle plan had broken down into a series of bloody skirmishes. But by mid-morning the Anzac force had advanced as far as a mile inland.

And that was when the bravery of the Anzacs was betrayed by the incompetence of their leaders. The Commander-in-Chief of the entire Gallipoli expedition was General Sir Ian Hamilton, an ageing, ineffectual leader who decided to run the operation from the comfort of the battleship *Queen Elizabeth* three miles off-shore, completely out of touch with his two corps commanders and the men on the beaches. Not that the corps commanders themselves were on the beaches. They were ordered to command their operations from ships standing off-shore, and, because communications quickly broke down, they too had little idea of what was going on.

Commander of the Anzac corps was General Sir William Birdwood, able and resourceful, but hampered by his unworkable orders. The other corps commander was General Sir Hunter Weston, in charge of the 29th Division of British and French troops, in whom Hamilton pinned his main hopes. Weston's men were landed on five beaches on Cape Helles, at the tip of the Gallipoli peninsula. They also carried out two decoy operations to divert Turkish troops into other areas miles away from the main front.

At Cape Helles, the first force of 2,000 British soldiers approached the shore inside an innocent-looking collier, the *River Clyde*, which was run aground on Sedd-el-Bahr beach. The attack was launched more than an hour after the Anzac landing. The British came ashore in broad daylight and ran into a hail of bullets from the waiting, well-entrenched Turks. Hundreds of men were shot dead as they crowded like sardines on the gangways that led ashore from the collier. The few who got on to the beach were picked off one by one as they scurried around seeking some shelter from the incessant enemy guns.

Four hours after the first landing, only about 200 Britons had scrambled ashore and survived. The pilot of a spotter plane which flew over the beach that morning described the sea as 'a horrible sight – absolutely red with blood'. The battle of Sedd-el-Bahr was lost before it was begun.

THE WORLD'S GREATEST MISTAKES

Within a stretch of a few miles, four other assaults had been launched on Cape Helles, and these had more success. On three beaches, the British troops landed and met little resistance, so they captured the commanding hillsides and sat down waiting for further orders. They never came.

On the other beach, Y Beach, there was no resistance at all. Two thousand men landed, climbed the cliffs and wandered around the prickly scrub unhindered. They sat on the hilltops and listened to the sound of their comrades being annihilated just an hour's march away. The Y Beach troops outnumbered the entire Turkish force in Cape Helles. They could have encircled and overrun the enemy that very day. But when their officers asked for permission to advance, the plea was refused.

The 2,000 men who had landed on Y Beach sat and waited for further orders throughout the whole of that bloody day. Until, in the evening, Turkish reinforcements arrived on the scene – and attacked them. The Britons, who had expected at any moment to be given orders to march onward, had not bothered to dig themselves in against an attack. And when that attack came, half of the invaders began to file back to the water's edge, where they came under fire. Since there was no word from their senior officers, these troops now took to their boats and began to evacuate Y Beach.

Meanwhile, the other half of the Y Beach force had pushed further inland, where they fought throughout the night. At dawn the next day they found that they were alone and unsupported, but they fought so well that by midmorning the Turks had fled.

Yet the great chance of victory was gone. The Allies in Cape Helles had outnumbered the Turkish defenders six to one, yet because there was no senior officer who could order a combined attack, the Allies had failed to press home their advantage. The Turks withdrew, but so did the British. The result was stalemate.

The only part of the whole operation which could be classed as a success was the French diversion on the other side of the Dardanelles Strait, at Kum Kale. There, with a regiment of African colonial troops, the French, in hand-

---

A tourist in Stockholm could not catch the restaurant waiter's eye, so he stepped outside, took all his clothes off and re-entered shouting: 'You Swedes only pay attention to nudes. Now will you serve me?' He was arrested for indecent behaviour.

to-hand fighting, had captured a major Turkish fort guarding the entrance to the Strait. The Turks had fled. But, in their moment of victory, the French had been ordered to withdraw and sail to Cape Helles. Kum Kale was, after all, just a diversion.

By midday on April 26, no fewer than 30,000 men had been landed on the Gallipoli peninsula . . . and none of them had been allowed by their leaders to achieve the victory that was in their grasp.

The original Anzacs had been reinforced by a further 15,000 men. But the enemy had not wasted their time either, and the main Turkish force was now concentrated on the hills around the Anzacs. By dusk of that day, the Anzac corps were all under siege on one tiny beach, without cover. At midnight Birdwood managed to get a message through to Hamilton's battleship asking for permission to evacuate his force.

He reported: 'My divisional generals and brigadiers have represented to me that they fear their men are thoroughly disorganised by shrapnel fire to which they have been subjected all day after exhausting and gallant work in the morning. Numbers have dribbled back from the firing line and cannot be collected in this difficult country. Even the New Zealand Brigade, which has only recently been engaged, lost heavily and is to some extent demoralised. If troops are subjected to shellfire again tomorrow there is likely to be a fiasco, as I have no fresh troops with which to replace those in the firing line. I know my representation is most serious but if we are to re-embark it must be at once.'

Thousands of lives could have been saved at that moment as Hamilton studied Birdwood's words aboard the battleship. But the tide of events turned on a second message that Hamilton received before he had made up his mind how to answer the first one.

This second report was from Lieutenant-Commander Huw Dacre Stoker, captain of the Australian submarine AE2. He had entered the Dardanelles Strait and, remaining on the surface to maintain his batteries, had passed into the Narrows under the guns of the Turkish forts. Shellfire made him submerge and he decided to pass beneath the Turks' floating minefield. He had to risk his submarine by surfacing twice in the middle of the minefield to check his position, and each time shells exploded around the craft. Finally Stoker came upon the main Turkish naval force sheltering behind the minefield, and he fired a torpedo at one of the cruisers, crash-diving just before the cruiser was able to ram him. But the torpedo hit home. Stoker kept the AE2 on the bottom for 16 hours, reading prayers to his men because it was a Sunday. Eventually, as the Turks gave up their hunt for the sub, he headed back down the Strait and radioed his success to the flagship *Queen Elizabeth*.

The vacillating Hamilton received the message and seized upon the only hopeful news of the day. He decided to send this reply to Birdwood's earlier

> **The court was told that soon after the party came into Maloney's Bar, Milligan spat at O'Flaherty and called him 'a stinking Ulsterman'. O'Flaherty punched Milligan, and Rourke hit him with a bottle. Milligan kicked O'Flaherty in the groin and threw a pint of beer in Rourke's face. This led to ill-feeling, and they began to fight.**
>
> – County Louth (Eire) newspaper

appeal for an evacuation:

'Your news is indeed serious. But there is nothing for it but to dig yourselves right in and stick it out. It would take at least two days to re-embark you. Meanwhile, an Australian submarine has got up through the Narrows and has torpedoed a gunboat. Hunter Weston, despite his heavy losses, will be advancing tomorrow, which should divert pressure from you. Make a personal appeal to your men to make a supreme effort to hold their ground. You have got through the difficult business. Now you have only to dig, dig, dig until you are safe.'

And dig, dig, dig they did. With the 100-yard beach littered with 2,000 casualties and the hills above them covered with about as many Turks, the Anzac troops dug their burrows into the cliffsides, and the enemy did the same. The grand Gallipoli plan had, within hours of being launched, settled down into the same appalling system of trench warfare that was wasting millions of lives in the fields of France.

The men at Anzac Cove and Cape Helles were to stay in those trenches and dug-outs for eight more months, and the Allied casualties were to climb to a quarter of a million before the pride of their leaders was sufficiently deflated to allow them to admit defeat and pull out.

By April 29, news got back to London that the Gallipoli offensive was not proving as successful as had been hoped. The news did not come from Hamilton, who prevaricated as his assault became bogged down. The news of the impending disaster was relayed instead by the Royal Navy.

Reinforcements were urgently needed – and they were available. In Egypt, where the original force had been assembled, fresh troops idly stood by, waiting for the call to sail to Gallipoli. But Hamilton never called them – either because he did not know they were available to him, or because of his pride. No one knows. Eventually, the reinforcements did sail, under direct orders from London. But by then the Turks too had summoned their best regiments to the narrow front.

Two weeks after the landings, Weston had lost 6,500 men at Cape Helles and had achieved nothing. Men were dying from lack of medical care, and ammunition was perilously low. Bayonet attacks and small sallies across trenches, producing heavy casualties, were the order of the day.

The scene at Anzac Cove was, if anything, worse. Each man was rationed to two bullets a day unless under prolonged attack. Along the ragged front lines, the opposing trenches were in some places less than 30 feet apart. Men lived like rats in holes in the hills, while on the beaches the maimed died on their stretchers under the constant barrage of Turkish shells.

On May 18 there took place at Anzac Cove the bloodiest battle of the campaign. The Turks had brought in fresh forces and now outnumbered by three to one the remaining 12,000 Australians and New Zealanders still able to fight. At 5 p.m. the greatest artillery barrage the Anzacs had yet seen burst around them. It continued into the night as the beleaguered soldiers huddled in their burrows. At 3 a.m. Birdwood ordered all his men to stand by for an expected attack. No sooner had they taken up their positions than the firing ceased. The front lines fell silent. There was a single bugle call – and a solid mass of Turks left their trenches and descended on the Anzacs. Wave after wave of Turks entered no-man's-land and were mown down before they could cross the narrow gap. The few who did cross were bayonetted as they fell into the Anzac trenches. The charges continued throughout the night and right through until midday. Every time a wave of Turks fell before the concerted fire of the Allies, another wave rose from the parapets of their trenches and charged to their deaths.

When the Turkish commanders called off the attacks, 10,000 of their men had fallen, half of them only yards from the Anzac trenches.

In the hours and days that followed, as both sides retreated to their trenches, the lines again fell relatively quiet. But throughout the day and night came moans and screams from those who had fallen in no-man's-land. With so many bodies putrefying, the danger of disease increased daily, and the Anzacs pressed Hamilton to negotiate a ceasefire so that the dead could be buried. Hamilton

---

A glossy American cookbook contained a recipe for Silky Caramel Slices: put an unopened can of condensed milk in a pot and leave it on the stove for four hours. The publishers later recalled all the books at vast expense, when they realised they had just invented the first exploding pudding - they had forgotten to mention that the pot should first be filled with water.

---

refused, saying that the request must come from the Turks.

But on May 20 the volunteer soldiers from Down Under took matters into their own hands, and raised a Red Cross flag above the front line. It was immediately shot at by the Turks, and the flagstaff was shattered. Then the most extraordinary thing happened. . . .

It was certain death to raise your head above the trenches of the front lines. Yet a lone Turkish soldier leaped up and began running across no-man's-land towards the Australians. He stopped above their trench and, in stumbling French, apologised for the shooting. Then he ran back again. Minutes later, Red Crescent flags appeared above the enemy trenches. General Walker, Commander of the 1st Australian Division, stood up and began slowly walking towards the Turkish lines. Not a shot was fired. Five Turkish officers came forward to greet him and they all chatted in French, exchanging pleasantries and cigarettes. After about ten minutes they parted, agreeing to meet again that evening to discuss an amnesty.

On May 24 there was a 'suspension of arms' so that each side could bury its dead. The enemies stood shoulder to shoulder and dug mass graves, all under the direction of Australian officers. Author Compton Mackenzie, who was an officer on Hamilton's staff, came ashore for the day and described the scene. 'Everywhere Turks were digging and digging graves for their countrymen who had been putrefying in heaps in the warm May air. The impression that scene made on my mind has obliterated all the rest of the time at Anzac. I cannot recall a single incident on the way back down the valley. I know only that nothing could cleanse the smell of death from the nostrils for a fortnight afterwards. There was no herb so aromatic but it reeked of carrion.'*

The truce was to end at 4.30 p.m. on May 24, and about half an hour before the deadline Turkish and Allied troops exchanged cigarettes and fruit and small gifts. They shook hands, parted with wide grins and returned to their

* *Gallipoli Memories* by Compton Mackenzie (Cassell, London)

Mr. Michael Vanner, of Bexhill Road, St. Leonards, a defendant in a recent case at Hastings Magistrates' Court, wishes to state that Mr. Melvin Peck, whom he pleaded not guilty to assaulting, was not a passer-by, as stated, but a friend of his.

       – Sussex newspaper

> In the Nuts (unground) (other than ground nuts) Order, the
> expression nuts shall have reference to such nuts, other
> than ground nuts, as would but for this amending Order
> not qualify as nuts (unground) (other than ground nuts) by
> reason of their being nuts (unground).
> – Amendment to British Parliamentary Act

own trenches. Shortly after 4.30, a Turkish sniper opened fire and the Anzacs blasted back. The war had begun again.

There was little respite for the next seven months. On August 6 Hamilton launched a fresh assault on Suvla Bay, north of the Anzac positions. The enemy was totally outflanked and fell back in disarray. By the end of the day, the Turks in the area were outnumbered 15 to one. But again the orders to push forward did not come. The Turks regrouped and sealed off the beachhead. It was the same old story: stalemate.

As 1915 dragged on, life became a living hell for the men on Cape Helles. Dysentery spread through the army, and 1,000 soldiers a week were shipped out suffering from it. Three-quarters of the Anzacs were seriously affected by it. More than half of them also suffered from skin sores through living in filthy trenches. The food was bad. And there was no fresh water in Anzac Cove – it had to be shipped from Egypt 750 miles away. Throughout the summer, there was a plague of flies over the camp, which helped spread disease. And finally the winter produced a new horror – frostbite for 15,000 soldiers.

In October the disastrous Hamilton was recalled and General Sir Charles Monro took over. He reported to the War Cabinet in London: 'The troops on the peninsula, with the exception of the Australian and New Zealand Corps, are not equal to a sustained effort owing to the inexperience of the officers, the want of training in the men and the depleted condition of many of the units. I am therefore of the opinion that another attempt to carry the Turkish lines would not offer any hope of success. On purely military grounds, I recommend the evacuation of the peninsula.'

The politicians argued the matter over until the middle of November before finally agreeing to give up the grand plan. Churchill resigned. He described Monro's part in the campaign thus: 'He came, he saw, he capitulated.'

Suvla Bay and Anzac Cove were evacuated in December 1915, and Cape Helles early the following month. One of the costliest blunders in history had come to an end. Half a million Allied troops had fought half a million Turks for eight months. And the result was 252,000 Allied casualties and 251,000 Turkish casualties. Even in death and injury there was stalemate.

U.S. *Arizona* after the Japanese attack.

Fiasco at Pearl Harbor

Warnings that were ignored could have prevented disaster

December 7, 1941, is a date that will for ever strike bitterness into the hearts of Americans. It was described by President Franklin D. Roosevelt as 'a date which will live in infamy' – the date on which Japanese aircraft swept out of the blue to bomb the pride of the American Pacific Fleet in Pearl Harbor.

The planes – almost 400 of them, launched from a vast carrier strike force – caused unimaginable damage, havoc and death on the wholly unprepared Hawaiian island of Oahu. But their coming had not been without warnings that, had they been heeded, would have at least halved the damage and the death toll that day.

The Japanese masterplan to cripple American opposition in the Pacific started being put into operation in mid-November of 1941. American agents in Japan reported that, one by one, major ships of the imperial navy had slipped out of their home ports and disappeared. The ships were assembling in Tankan Bay, along the string of islands that stretched into the icy waters of northern Japan.

From there, on November 26, sailed a vast force: six aircraft carriers, two battleships, three cruisers, nine destroyers, eight tankers and three submarines. An advance force of about 25 submarines, five of them carrying midget submarines, had gone ahead.

The main force had a journey ahead of it stretching halfway across the Pacific Ocean, and it was vital to the success of its mission that no one else should even know of its existence. To this end, radio silence was maintained, no garbage was dumped overboard, only low-smoke fuel was used, and there was a strict black-out. The cover-up was taken to such limits that ships remaining in Japanese home waters increased their own level of radio communications to a constant chatter in order to persuade U.S. eavesdroppers that the full fleet was still in the area.

On December 1, a mysterious message was broadcast from Tokyo. It was simply: 'Climb Mount Niitaka'. Only the commander of the strike fleet, Vice-Admiral Chuichi Nagumo, knew what it meant: the Imperial Council had decided on war, and the attack on Pearl Harbor was to proceed. Even so, the commander's instructions were that if the fleet were to be spotted on any day up to or including December 6, it should turn back, having lost the element of surprise. If it were sighted on December 7, the commander of the strike force would decide whether the attack should still go ahead – at 0800 hours, Sunday, December 7.

Apart from the strange disappearance from port of so many ships of the Japanese Navy, the first warning that could have helped the American authorities avert a major disaster at Pearl Harbor came on December 5. The local FBI branch in Hawaii tapped a phone call between Tokyo and a Japanese dentist living in Honolulu. The conversation ranged over the subjects of aircraft, defences and the number of ships in Pearl Harbor. But most of the time was spent talking about flowers. 'The hibiscus and poinsettia are now in bloom,' was how the conversation ended. The message was thought to be a code, but no great weight was attached to it. After all, a Japanese attack on Pearl Harbor was out of the question. Washington had warned that a declaration of war was expected from the Japanese, but an attack was believed to be coming in the Far East – probably in Borneo or the Philippines.

Washington had been well alerted to the possibility of war. The Americans had broken the secret code used in messages between Tokyo and the Japanese Embassy in Washington, and they had translated a long declaration that was evidently destined to be handed over by the Japanese envoys. The final part of the document, actually declaring war on the United States, would have completed the message that would plummet the Americans into World War Two. The curious Japanese sense of honour would have been satisfied if the declaration had been presented just before their strike force hit Hawaii. But it was not received from Tokyo in time.

So, on the morning of December 7, the Americans on the Hawaiian islands were not alerted to the fact that they could be a target for the Japanese. There had been mildly voiced fears of sabotage by the large Japanese civilian population of Hawaii if war were declared. But Pearl Harbor in the front line? Never!

Early in the morning of December 7 American military personnel went to bed after Honolulu's Saturday night parties and dances, while two dozen submarines of the Japanese advance force closed in around Pearl Harbor. Their job was to torpedo any ships that tried to escape the airborne attack that was about to be launched. From five of the subs, two-man midget submarines, each bearing twin torpedoes, were to be launched against warships inside the harbour at the same time as the planes.

Then came another of the warnings that should have alerted the Americans. At 3.30 a.m. the minesweeper *Condor* sighted a submarine periscope heading towards the entrance to Pearl Harbor. The *Condor*, which was patrolling just outside the harbour, signalled the destroyer *Ward*, which was on duty nearby. Battle stations were called and held for an hour, but the submarine was not sighted again.

Shortly before 5 a.m., the *Condor* went off duty. The anti-submarine net across the harbour mouth was drawn open to allow the vessel back inside. The net was not closed again because other ships were expected to be moving in and out of the harbour over the next few hours. Pearl Harbor was wide open to the midget submarines which were even then moving towards the 96 warships lying snugly inside. The net was left open because neither the *Condor* nor the *Ward* reported to shore that a submarine was in the area.

At 6 a.m., in high seas 250 miles north of Oahu, six Japanese aircraft carriers turned their bows into the wind and a swarm of aircraft, laden with bombs and torpedoes, roared into the dawn sky to the cheers of the crews. The plan was to

---

> **Delays and confusion mean that solicitors either have to work for nothing or tell an inarticulate client that he must conduct his own ass.**
>
> – *Times*

Pearl Harbor at the height of the fire.

launch 350 planes in two waves, one at 6 a.m. and the other at 7 a.m. Another 80 planes were split between reconnaisance missions, defence of the fleet and reserves.

Most of Pearl Harbor still slumbered. But at 6.45 a.m. the first shot of the battle was fired. The destroyer *Ward*, still on patrol, spotted a midget submarine at the harbour entrance and opened fire on it. Then it ran at the sub as if to ram it, dropped a depth charge as it passed – and blew it up. A quarter of an hour later a second sub was sighted. More depth charges were dropped and this sub, too, was thought to have been destroyed. It was shortly after 7 a.m. that the second wave of Japanese planes took off from the carriers to the north. But in Pearl Harbor the only concern was that the early-morning 'exercises' taking place off-shore were not helping the hangovers suffered by the sleepy party-goers of the previous night.

The *Ward* radioed ashore to report the encounters with the submarines, in two messages, both in code. But it was at 7.15 a.m. that, because of delays in decoding, the first message reached the only man on duty at U.S. naval headquarters at Pearl Harbor. He was a veteran reservist, Lieutenant-Commander Harold Kaminsky, who spent the next 20 minutes raising some

THE WORLD'S GREATEST MISTAKES

of the navy top brass at their homes. But aboard the warships in Pearl Harbor, all anyone was concerned with was the hoisting of the morning colours.

Another wasted warning had come just before 7 a.m. Army radar stations on Oahu picked up the blips of two aircraft heading in from the north. They were probably Japanese reconnaissance aircraft flying ahead of the first wave of dive-bombers and torpedo planes. The reports went into the island's information centre for plotting. Unfortunately, at 7 a.m. everything stopped for breakfast, and this one-hour warning of impending disaster was also ignored.

At 7.05 a.m. Opana radar station on the northern tip of Oahu island picked up the first clear-cut sign that a major attack was about to take place. Dozens of aircraft showed up on the screen. The men at Opana were also supposed to have stood down at 7 a.m. but they stayed on duty to track the vast formation which was now only 100 miles away and closing fast. Bewildered, they put through reports to the information centre. But the centre had virtually closed down for breakfast, and the only two men on duty were the switchboard operator and one officer who was waiting to be relieved so that he too could get his coffee and a bite to eat. The men at Opana became fed up with passing through reports that were seemingly being ignored, so they also packed up and went off for breakfast.

The first wave of Japanese planes was now over the coast.

On the battleship *Nevada* lying in Pearl Harbor the ship's band began playing *The Star Spangled Banner* as part of the regular Sunday morning ceremony of hoisting the colours. Just then, a plane with a bright red circle on each wingtip swooped out of the sky, dropped a torpedo and skimmed over the *Nevada*'s decks. The plane's rear-gunner fired on the bandsmen but succeeded only in shredding the American flag to tatters. The band finished playing then fled for cover. The attack on Pearl Harbor had begun. It was 7.55 a.m.

At 8 a.m. a message was radioed to Washington, to the Atlantic and Pacific Fleets and all U.S. warships at sea: 'Air raid on Pearl Harbor – this is no drill.'

For the next two hours, wave upon wave of bombers, dive-bombers and torpedo aircraft pummelled Pearl Harbor and its surrounding air bases. Almost 200 American planes were destroyed, most of them on the ground. In the middle of the attack a flight of U.S. B-17 bombers arrived over Oahu on a routine mission. They found themselves in a maelstrom, were shot up, and crash-landed wherever they could.

The Japanese lost 30 aircraft, as well as all five of their midget submarines and one of the large subs. Fewer than 100 men in all. Their losses were so low because they had maintained the element of surprise. As for the Americans, having failed to read the warning signs, their losses were huge by contrast.

In Pearl Harbor itself, thick black smoke from a sea of burning oil obscured the carnage. Five torpedoes slammed into the battleship *Oklahoma*. It turned turtle. Its sister ship, the *Arizona*, exploded spectacularly from a direct bomb hit and sank, entombing 1,100 men. Three other battleships were seriously damaged but later salvaged. The *West Virginia* was hit by six torpedoes and sank. The *California* was hit by two torpedoes. The blazing *Nevada*, with a torpedo in its side and two bomb hits, made a dash for the harbour mouth but ran aground. The battleships *Tennessee*, *Pennsylvania* and *Maryland* were also damaged.

The target ship *Utah* was torpedoed and capsized. The cruiser *Helena* suffered the same fate. The minelayer *Oglala* was sunk by the same torpedo that holed the *Helena*. The destroyer *Shaw* exploded in dry dock. Its sister ships *Cassin* and *Downes* were totally destroyed in dry dock. The cruiser *Raleigh* was holed but remained afloat. The cruiser *Honolulu* was put out of action.

Eight miles away, the city that the *Honolulu* was named after suffered only mild damage. It was hit by one Japanese bomb – and about 40 U.S. Navy shells fired by ships in harbour at the attacking aircraft.

Sixty-eight civilians died that day and 2,335 American servicemen – almost half of them lost aboard the battleship *Arizona*.

Shortly after 3 p.m. on the afternoon of the attack, a cable from Washington was delivered to Lieutenant-General Walter C. Short, commander of the U.S. Army ground and air forces in Hawaii. Its message was that the Japanese were planning to present an official declaration at 7.30 Honolulu time that morning. It added: 'Just what significance the hour set may have we do not know – but be on the alert.' This warning would have been delivered to General Short earlier but it had been delayed because of the need to decode it, because of the air attack and because it was a Sunday. The cable had been received at 7.33 that morning.

Firemen paraded proudly for the opening of their showpiece headquarters at Barnsley, Yorkshire. Then factory inspectors moved in and ordered a vital addition to the building – a fire escape.

Massacre of the Light Brigade

The tragic charge into the Valley of Death by 'the noble six hundred'

C'est magnifique, mais ce n'est pas la guerre' ('It's magnificent, but it isn't war'). The remark was made by French General Bosquet as he watched the famous Light Brigade of the British Army charge to their destruction in the Crimea in 1854. And the comment has gone down in history as the truest verdict on a spectacular blunder that both shocked and inspired a nation.

The Charge of the Light Brigade resulted from the enmity, jealousy, suspicion and, above all, the conflicting pride of three men.

Lord Raglan, a soldier since the age of 15, was supreme commander. He was a popular leader and had served at Waterloo 39 years earlier, when he had watched with clenched teeth as a field surgeon amputated his right arm.

Under his command was Lord Lucan, who, as the young George Bingham, had bought himself the command of the 17th Lancers and had proved himself such a stickler for dress and discipline that his men were called Bingham's Dandies. He was tireless and brave but uninspiring, and he was hated by his officers for his pettiness and by his men for the floggings he was so keen to order.

No one hated Lucan more than his brother-in-law, Lord Cardigan, who commanded the 11th Hussars. They spoke hardly a word to each other. Cardigan had seen little war service, was also an enthusiast for floggings, and isolated himself from his officers by living aboard his private yacht off Balaclava. Yet he was a more flamboyant and colourful character than his brother-in-law and he inspired strong loyalty in the ranks.

The ill-fated Charge of the Light Brigade took place shortly after an earlier attack by the rival Heavy Brigade. The riders of the Heavy Brigade had routed an overwhelmingly superior force of Russian cavalry near Balaclava. The generals commanding the Light Brigade had watched the Heavy Brigade in action, but had been denied permission to join in and complete the rout. They felt cheated of a share in the glory.

After the Heavy Brigade's action, the Russian forces regrouped at the end of a long narrow valley which was bounded on two sides by hills, at the western end by the Chersonese Plateau and at the eastern end by the River Tchernaya. The Russian cavalry was drawn up at the eastern end of the valley, behind a solid line of cannons. Russian artillery flanked the valley in commanding positions on both sides – on the Fedioukine Hills to the north and the Causeway Heights to the south.

The Russians had already been driven out of some of their previously held positions on the Causeway Heights, and the British infantry, along with their French allies, were preparing to evict them from the others. Raglan, whose headquarters were on the Chersonese Plateau, had a clear view down the length of the valley and could see clearly how the battle lines were shaping up.

Raglan decided that his infantry should winkle the enemy out of their emplacements on the hills while his cavalry should enter the valley to attack

---

The chairman reported that Bradford Council would not be able to repaint yellow No Parking lines in the village until the man who did the job had used up all the white paint in his bucket.

– Yorkshire newspaper

---

the retreating Russians as, one by one, the small pockets of resistance gave out. The plan was logical – the enemy gunners would be forced down from the hills on to the valley floor and the Light Brigade would pick them off with impunity.

But that was not how it happened.

On the southern side of the valley, the 1st Division of infantry advanced towards the Causeway Heights. On the other side, the 4th Division also advanced, but much more slowly. In the middle, the 600-strong Light Brigade, raring for action after jealously watching the success of the Heavy Brigade, moved forward too.

> *Half a league, half a league,*
> *Half a league onward,*
> *All in the valley of Death*
> *Rode the six hundred.*

So begins the famous poem by Alfred, Lord Tennyson, which describes the action and has immortalised the brave cavalrymen who took part in it.

The Light Brigade were far ahead of the infantry, and historians have argued that they should have been ordered to wait until the 1st and 4th Divisions caught up with them. But, due to a series of misunderstandings, they were launched on a spectacular but insane course of action.

The catalogue of chronic blunders began when Raglan, from his vantage point high on the Chersonese Plateau, saw that the Russians had already begun to pull out of some of their positions on the Causeway Heights and were hauling their cannon down the valley to the safety of their main force. There was no need for the British infantry to winkle them out – they were already sitting targets for the cavalry.

Raglan issued his first order to the Light Brigade: 'Advance and take advantage of any opportunity to recover the Heights. You will be supported by the infantry.'

Lucan received the order by messenger and thought it characteristically vague, which indeed it was. He interpreted it to mean that he was to wait for the infantry. So he moved the Light Brigade to the head of the valley, ordered a halt . . . and waited.

Raglan spluttered with rage and impatience when he saw the cavalry idling on the valley floor. He watched through his telescope as the Russians moved around without hindrance at the far end of the valley. Raglan called for his chief of staff, General Airey, and asked him to send off a further order to Lucan.

This order Airey took down on a flimsy scrap of paper as he stood before

the supreme commander. The order was: 'Advance rapidly to the front to prevent the enemy from carrying away their guns.' Airey gave the vital scrap of paper to his own aide de camp, Captain Nolan, and as Nolan wheeled his horse around to deliver the note personally to Lucan, Raglan shouted after him: 'Tell him to attack instantly.'

Nolan sent his horse slithering down the precipitous slopes to the valley below to pass the crucial message to Lucan, a leader whom he despised for his superior airs and inferior experience. Eventually, his horse bathed in sweat and dust, Nolan drew up alongside Lucan's horse and passed over the now-grimy slip of paper.

Lucan read the note nonchalantly and put it aside. He commented lightly that it seemed a foolhardy order, and he leaned back in his saddle to contemplate the situation as if he had all the time in the world.

This was too much for the fiery Nolan, an outspoken individualist but respected by his superiors as a battle-hardened officer.

'My Lord,' shouted Nolan, 'the orders are for the cavalry to attack instantly.'

Lucan was taken aback. He rounded angrily on his junior officer and remonstrated: 'Attack? Attack what? What guns?'

Nolan lost all patience. He pointed down the valley and shouted: 'There, my Lord, is your enemy. There are the guns.'

But Nolan was not pointing at the struggling Russians trying to pull their artillery out of their isolated positions on the Causeway Heights. He was pointing straight down the long valley to the massed Russian forces at the far end.

Dismissively, Lucan shrugged his shoulders and turned his horse away. He trotted over to his brother-in-law and ordered him to attack the Russian artillery immediately. Cardigan remonstrated with him, but the conversation was curt and unproductive.

'Allow me to point out, sir,' said Cardigan, 'that the enemy have a battery in the valley in our front and batteries and riflemen on both flanks.'

Lucan replied: 'I know it, but Raglan will have it. We must obey. Advance steadily.'

Lucan rode back to brigade headquarters. Cardigan rode off to rally his officers.

Cardigan drew up the Light Brigade at the head of the valley. On the right he placed the 13th Light Dragoons. On the left was Lucan's regiment, the 17th Lancers (in the temporary command of Captain Morris, while Lucan stood by with the Heavy Brigade). Cardigan's regiment, the 11th Hussars, formed a second line of cavalry. In the rear, the 8th Hussars and the 4th Light Dragoons formed up under Lord George Paget.

Up front, Cardigan ordered: 'Sound the advance', and a trumpeter sent the 607 horses first into a walk and then into a trot.

> 'Forward the Light Brigade!
> Charge for the guns!' he said:
> Into the valley of Death
> Rode the six hundred.

Cardigan was out in front of the brigade on his chestnut charger. Nolan, the man who had passed on the fatal orders to Lucan, was nearby. He had asked to be allowed to ride with the 17th Lancers. When he realised the direction in which the brigade was heading, he left his place in the ranks and galloped forward to warn Cardigan of the error, but almost as soon as he reached the head of the mass of men and horses a Russian shell burst near him. Shrapnel hit Nolan in the chest and he and his horse collapsed in the dust.

The trumpeter, riding next to Cardigan, was ordered to sound the gallop. He had barely done so when he too was killed.

The Russian guns on the riders' flanks were now firing incessantly and the leading lancers were already falling like flies. But the target of the charge, the

THE WORLD'S GREATEST MISTAKES

main body of the Russian force, was still more than a mile away. . . .

> 'Forward the Light Brigade!'
> Was there a man dismay'd?
> Not tho' the soldier knew
> Some one had blunder'd:
> Their's not to make reply,
> Their's not to reason why,
> Their's but to do and die:
> Into the valley of Death
> Rode the six hundred.

There was now no trumpeter to sound the charge. But the eagerness of the men to pass through the rain of bullets and shells and reach the end of the valley as quickly as possible forced the pace. The charge began unordered.

'Steady the 17th Lancers,' called Cardigan as his men threatened to overtake their leader. Riders and horses fell one after another but the lines were immediately closed and the solid mass of men and chargers galloped up the dusty valley floor. Some horses, by now riderless, continued to charge until they too were hit.

> Cannon to right of them,
> Cannon to left of them,
> Cannon in front of them
> Volley'd and thunder'd;
> Storm'd at with shot and shell,
> Boldly they rode and well,
> Into the jaws of Death,
> Into the mouth of Hell
> Rode the six hundred.

The hail of shot and shell had become a murderous crossfire as the brigade was fired on from three sides. One man had his head cleanly severed but his torso continued in the saddle, his lance still pointing ahead to its target. Cannon fire began to knock out as many as four chargers at a time. One horse tore out its own entrails with its galloping hooves.

Suddenly the dust and smoke thickened and Cardigan, still at the head of his men, vanished into the midst of it. The Light Brigade were upon the Russian guns. Lances struck home, swords cut down the enemy gunners.

The brigade swept through the guns and into the thick of the waiting cavalry ranked behind them. The fighting was wholly disordered. Cardigan was involved in a hand-to-hand skirmish with a dozen Cossacks. But many of the British swept clean through the enemy cavalry and then had to fight every

inch of their way back again. Many were captured.

> *Flash'd all their sabres bare,*
> *Flash'd as they turn'd in air*
> *Sabring the gunners there,*
> *Charging an army, while*
> *All the world wonder'd:*
> *Plunged in the battery-smoke*
> *Right thro' the line they broke;*
> *Cossack and Russian*
> *Reel'd from the sabre-stroke*
> *Shatter'd and sunder'd.*
> *Then they rode back, but not,*
> *Not the six hundred.*

The dreadful hail of death from three sides had to be faced all over again as the tattered remnants of the Light Brigade rode back up the valley towards

their own lines. But on the return journey there was an added hazard – they
were pursued by Hussars and Cossacks.

> *Cannon to right of them,*
> *Cannon to left of them,*
> *Cannon behind them*
> *Volley'd and thunder'd;*
> *Storm'd at with shot and shell,*
> *While horse and hero fell,*
> *They that had fought so well*
> *Came thro' the jaws of Death,*
> *Back from the mouth of Hell,*
> *All that was left of them*
> *Left of six hundred.*

Private John Wightman, whose father had been Cardigan's riding master,
was one of the survivors of the 17th Lancers. He left for the history books a
graphic account of the futile battle.

On the charge down the valley Wightman had been shot through the right
knee and shin but he refused to pull out and continued into the Russian lines,
where a Cossack stuck a lance through his right thigh. Wightman killed the
Cossack before he could do further damage. The private's horse was riddled
with bullets but Wightman managed to coax it back through the enemy lines
and 400 yards down the valley towards safety before it dropped dead.

As Wightman lay on the ground, a pursuing Cossack drove a lance at least
eight times into his neck, back and through his right hand. But Wightman
survived to spend the rest of the war as a prisoner.

Cardigan got back to his own lines and was cheered by his men. The main
blame for the whole terrible episode was laid on his hated brother-in-law.

Lucan had begun to lead the Heavy Brigade down the valley in support of
of the beleaguered Light Brigade but, seeing the futility of the effort, he drew
his men up and retired, himself wounded in the leg.

Cardigan was proclaimed a hero. He said: 'It was a mad-brained trick but
it was no fault of mine.'

**A tubby Chicago garbage collector, Ruffs Jackson, was
warned that he would be fired unless he slimmed. He
dutifully crash-dieted and lost 200 pounds. But that was not
all he lost. He fell ill, found that he could not lift the bins,
was given the sack anyway, and his wife fell out of love
with him.**

It was Tennyson who was to leave the most enduring tribute to the Light Brigade.

> *When can their glory fade?*
> *O the wild charge they made!*
> *All the world wonder'd.*
> *Honour the charge they made!*
> *Honour the Light Brigade,*
> *Noble six hundred!*

But for most of the Light Brigade, that tribute was also an epitaph. Of the 'noble six hundred', only 329 returned that day from the Valley of Death.

Mission of madness

Hitler's deputy flew to negotiate peace, but was branded a lunatic

It was meant to be the masterstroke to end World War Two. Rudolf Hess, Adolf Hitler's deputy, made a secret night flight from Germany in a lone fighter aircraft and parachuted into Scotland. He planned to meet King George VI to offer him peace in a pact between the two countries. But it all went dreadfully wrong.

Hess was taken prisoner as soon as he landed on British soil, and he has been a captive ever since. Now, at 85, he seems certain to die a prisoner in Berlin's Spandau Prison.

The bizarre story began on the night of May 10, 1941, when Hess obtained a Messerschmitt 110 fighter plane by saying that he needed it for long-range training flights inside Germany. After take-off, he headed out across the English Channel and then set a course for Scotland. At 11.07 p.m. a searchlight unit about eight miles south of Glasgow spotted Hess's unaccompanied aircraft. They watched as the plane circled the city twice with the engine switched off.

To their horror, they saw the aircraft go into a shallow dive – straight at them. The men manning the searchlight thought they were being dive-bombed. Then they saw a parachute stream out. The pilotless plane dived towards the light, then suddenly veered off, crashing about 250 yards away and bursting into flames.

Two anti-aircraft signalmen watched the pilot floating down to earth beneath his billowing canopy of white silk. Then they set off for where they thought he had landed – farmer Basil Baird's field at Eaglesham, a village eight miles south of Glasgow and close to the estate of the Duke of Hamilton. But by the time they reached the field, Hess had already made his first contact with the enemy – ploughman David McLean.

Farmer Baird was getting ready for bed when McLean rushed into his house and blurted out the astonishing news that a Nazi had parachuted into the field at the rear of the farm. McLean said that the mysterious German flyer's first words to him were: 'Excuse me, but would you please direct me to the Duke of Hamilton?'

Neither Baird nor McLean knew the identity of the jackbooted man wearing the blue-grey uniform of a Luftwaffe captain. It was not until two days later that they heard it announced on the radio that the man they had confronted was Hitler's deputy.

Shortly after Hess was taken into the cottage, the two anti-aircraft signalmen who had seen his descent arrived on the scene. They were met at the door by McLean, who told them: 'He's inside – he arrived about half a minute ago.'

The signalmen burst into the cottage and found the parachutist seated in an armchair. Showing them his empty hands, he said: 'Ah, British soldiers – no guns – no bombs.' He told them that his name was Alfred Horn.

'Where have you come from?' one of the soldiers asked. 'Munich, in four hours,' came the reply. Hess, who had a camera slung around his neck and a map with a roughly-plotted course strapped to his knee, said that he had never before been to Britain. But he added mysteriously: 'I have a very important message for the Duke of Hamilton.'

Hess was friendly with the soldiers, and showed them pictures of his wife and son, with whom he said he had spent that morning. Before he was marched away, he was offered a cup of tea, but asked instead for a glass of water.

Meanwhile, so many civilians had gathered around the scene of the crashed aircraft that the searchlight detachment had to fix bayonets to move them away from the wreckage. Many of the people attracted by the explosion managed to pocket souvenirs from the plane.

A 26-year-old man who parachuted into the middle of a four-lane highway near Joliet, Illinois, was arrested by police and charged with not using an authorised entrance.

Rudolf Hess with Hitler. *Inset* The Duke of Hamilton.

THE WORLD'S GREATEST MISTAKES

> **MONTY FLIES BACK TO FRONT.**
>
> *– Daily Mirror*

Hess was taken away, limping (he had landed awkwardly at the end of his parachute fall), and under escort, to the local Home Guard headquarters. There, a gunner who formed part of the escort suddenly thought there was something familiar about the face of the prisoner. He later scanned pictures in newspapers and magazines and pointed to a photograph of Hess. 'That's him,' he said. 'I'm sure that's him.' But to his comrades the idea seemed so preposterous that they laughed him into silence.

Eventually, a Royal Air Force intelligence officer began his interrogation of the parachutist, in front of other officers. After a while, one of the men, Major Graham Donald, of the Royal Observer Corps, told the interrogating officer: 'You know, sir, I believe this is Rudolf Hess. I've seen him in Germany before the war, and I recognise him as Hess.'

'Don't be a fool,' he was told. 'What would Hitler's deputy be doing in Scotland?'

Hess was later transferred to Maryhill Barracks, where he said he was on a special mission to the Duke of Hamilton, and that he had intended to land at Dungavel, 12 miles from the field where he parachuted down. Because of what had been said, the Duke of Hamilton, a wing commander in the Royal Air Force, visited Hess. At the German's request, the interrogating officer and the military officer on guard, who were also present, left Hess to talk alone with the duke. Hess then revealed for the first time his identity and explained that he had chosen to see the duke because they had lunched together at Hess's house during the 1936 Olympic Games in Berlin. Hess believed that the duke had sufficient influence to arrange a meeting with the King, with whom Hess would be able to arrange a negotiated peace.

Years later, in a Nuremberg jail, Hess told an American army psychiatrist: 'I flew to see the King. I wanted him to go to Germany for a peace conference with Hitler. I wanted to save the world from Bolshevism. I knew the Duke of Hamilton and thought he would take me to the King.'

Hess had previously sent letters to the duke, each one requesting a meeting, but the duke had immediately handed them to security forces and had sent no reply.

Hitler knew nothing of Hess's plan until it had been put into operation. When he learned of it he flew into a rage.

At the end of the war, Hermann Goering, head of the Luftwaffe, told the story of what happened: 'I saw Hitler reading the letter Hess had left for him. For a moment he sat limply, then he became furious, ordering the arrest of all who knew of the flight.'

But Hess had kept his secret well. Only two people knew of it – his secretary and his adjutant. He had not even told his wife about the plan.

'Hitler thought Hess had gone mad,' Goering said.

The Nazi propaganda machine churned out a series of conflicting stories in an attempt to explain away Hess's flight from Germany. They described him as a lunatic, an invalid seized by a brainstorm. Then he was made out to be the idealist and patriot – 'an angel of peace' – who had walked into an evil British trap.

At first, Berlin said that Hitler's deputy had no knowledge of German secrets, then announced the fervent hope that the British would be sufficiently chivalrous not to attempt to worm any secrets from him.

When the war was over and Hess was awaiting trial at Nuremberg with other war criminals, he gave the full story of his mission. He first planned his flight after Hitler had told him in June 1940: 'The basis of my policy upon seizing power must be an understanding with England. Even today, I have not yet given up this hope. I consider this war, in which for a second time within a generation the people of a noble race are decimating each other and destroying their very substance, as a terrible tragedy. The sooner it is ended the better. But in order to attain this end, everything must be avoided which might wound British prestige.'

Hess had reasoned 'that England would negotiate without loss of prestige only if she had a reason visible to the whole world for entering into talks with Germany . . . I therefore decided to supply this reason by going personally to England.

'The decision to go was the hardest I have ever made in my life. It was rendered easier, however, when I visualised the endless rows of coffins, both in Germany and in England, with mothers in dire distress following behind.

'I am convinced that mothers on both sides of the Channel will have understood my action.'

Shortly after Hess presented this first full public explanation of his bizarre flight, the international court at Nuremberg sentenced him to life imprisonment for 'planning aggressive war' from his position as Hitler's deputy.

From that time, Hess was held virtually in solitary confinement in Berlin's Spandau Prison. In 1967, he became the only inmate of the 600-cell jail. He was not officially allowed to speak to anyone other than his wife, Ilse, and son, Wolf, during their monthly visits. British, American, French and Soviet troops took turns guarding him during the last, lonely years of his life.

The mouse that roared too loudly

When Adolf Hitler ordered his engineers to develop a monster tank, they code-named the project The Mouse. Such a title for the most invulnerable instrument of war was the Germans' idea of a joke.

The Mouse was to be a land-borne battleship. It was 50 feet long, with impressive firepower, a 1,500 horse-power motor, and armour plating so thick that it could withstand a direct hit by another tank. It was also watertight and could cross rivers under water.

The only trouble was that, to fulfil all these requirements, the tank had to weigh 180 tons. And when, in 1944, its designer Dr. Porsche, of Volkswagen and sports-car fame, launched it on to the roads of Germany for its trials, it ploughed them up and made them impassable, cracked the foundations of buildings, smashed windows by its vibrations and, when it left the roads, sank into the ground.

The Mouse that roared too loudly was immediately scrapped.

A 22-year-old Los Angeles man advertised in a magazine as a lonely Romeo looking for a girl with whom to share a holiday tour of South America. The joyful Juliet who answered his plea turned out to be his widowed mother.

The man who never was

The body on the beach at Huelva meant little to the Spanish fisherman who had netted it from the sea. After all, this was April 1943, and World War Two had provided a steady flow of corpses from crashed planes and sunken ships in the Atlantic.

But this body was different. For this was the man who never was. And many Allied soldiers are still alive today because of the way he fooled the Germans.

The Allies had just driven the Nazis out of North Africa, and in the words of Winston Churchill, 'anybody but a damn fool' would know that Sicily must

> **The three things that make a good motorist are concentration and anticipation.**
>
> – *Sunday People*

be the next Allied target for invasion. Somehow, the Allies had to trick Hitler into thinking otherwise.

The answer, dreamed up by a top-secret Admiralty department, was brilliant. It was to provide the Nazis with documents they would never expect to get, and in a way that would never make them suspect a plot. . . .

A courier would be flying to North Africa with written instructions for the victorious Allied leaders. His plane would crash – and he and the documents would be washed up in Spain. Though nominally neutral, the Franco government had strong German sympathies, and there were enough Nazi agents in the country to make the Allies confident that any British documents would soon find their way to Berlin.

An actual plane crash was unnecessary. Anyway, planes lost at sea often left no surface debris. Instead, the body was to be put into the sea from a submarine off the Spanish coast.

Obtaining the fake documents was easy. First, General Sir Archibald Nye, Vice-chief of the Imperial General Staff, 'wrote to' General Alexander, commander of the 8th Army, 'revealing' plans to assault Cape Araxos, in Greece. Then Admiral Lord Louis Mountbatten 'wrote to' General Eisenhower, Supreme Commander in North Africa, and Sir Andrew Cunningham, Admiral of the Fleet, making a joke about sardines to make the Nazis think of Sardinia; in his 'letter' Mountbatten also introduced the courier as a trusted member of his staff at Combined Operations Headquarters.

But the real problem was finding a dead courier, and making him appear plausible to the Germans. It was decided that the man should be in his early thirties and must convincingly seem to have been the victim of an air crash at sea.

Eventually the body of a man of the right age was found. He had died of pneumonia after exposure. His parents agreed to allow their son to be used, as long as he later received proper burial, and on condition that his true identity was never revealed.

So the Admirality team set about creating a new identity for their man. They made him a Royal Marine, and called him Captain (Acting Major) William Martin, because there were several Martins in the marines. They listed him as having been born in Cardiff in 1907. And they gave him identity card No. 148228. To explain why the card looked so new, they added a handwritten line which read: Issued in lieu of No. 09650, lost.

Now they added some colour to the character they had created. Into his wallet went a £5 note and three £1 notes. Into his trouser pockets they put 5s. 10d. in change, a packet of cigarettes, a box of matches, a pencil stub, two used bus tickets and a bunch of keys, a receipted bill for a six-night stay at the Naval and Military Club in London's Piccadilly, and the stubs of two theatre tickets.

To give Major Martin a private life, an Admiralty girl wrote two letters to him as his fiancée. These, together with a snapshot of her and a bill for a £53 engagement ring, went into his pockets. So did a letter from his 'father', written from North Wales, in which news of his son's engagement was noted less than enthusiastically.

The final touches were a letter from Lloyds Bank, urging prompt action over a £79 overdraft, and a note from a firm of solicitors acknowledging instructions for his will.

All was now ready for delivery of the dead messenger. The corpse was brought out of cold storage, put into uniform and fitted with a lifejacket. His personal effects were packed and the official documents, in a briefcase, were strapped to his wrist. Finally, he went into a special container of dry ice, and two men set off with the corpse on the long overnight drive to Greenock, Scotland, where the submarine *Seraph* was waiting to sail for Malta.

At this stage, only the submarine's commanding officer was in on the secret. When the bulky canister, labelled 'optical instruments', went on board, the crew were told that it contained a special weather-checking buoy which was to be put into the sea off Spain without the Spanish knowing about it.

After ten days at sea, the *Seraph* surfaced off the south coast of Spain at 4.30 a.m. on April 30. Traces of mist swirled across a calm sea as selected officers, told the true nature of their cargo only at the last minute, carried the canister on deck. They took out Major Martin, inflated his Mae West jacket and slid him gently into the water a mile from the mouth of the Huelva River. A rubber dinghy and a paddle went in after him, to add evidence of an air crash.

The plan could not have worked better. The Spanish fisherman reported his find that same morning, and the body was handed over to a Spanish naval

> **All meat in this window is from local farmers killed on the premises.**
>
> – sign in Somerset butcher's shop

Lord Mountbatten.

patrol. News of the 'tragedy' soon reached the British Embassy in Madrid, along with the major's personal effects. But there was no word of the documents.

It took an alarmed formal demand for their return from London before they were handed back on May 13. And by then they had done their job. Scientific tests proved that the envelopes had been opened. And after the war, captured Nazi documents showed that the letters had been studied at the highest level, convincing even Hitler that the Allied assault would be on Greece and Sardinia.

The German High Command scattered their forces, ready – as they thought – to surprise the invaders. But it was they who received the shock when the Allies stormed Sicily and found themselves opposed by only one Italian and two German divisions.

The invasion was successful, losses on the beaches were far lighter than expected, and a path had been carved into Europe via Italy.

But the hero of the hour was the one man who knew nothing about it. The man who never was. The man who had been buried with full military honours at Huelva by the very people who had unwittingly helped him to bamboozle Hitler.

One-man war

Jungle soldier fought on for 29 years

On August 6, 1945, an atomic bomb exploded over Hiroshima. Three-quarters of the city was destroyed and almost 80,000 people died. Four days later, Nagasaki was also laid waste by an atomic bomb. On August 14, Japan surrendered – and World War Two came to an end.

Soldiers of all nations, who for years had faced deprivation and danger, returned to their homes and their families. But all over the Pacific, on tiny, remote islands, pockets of Japanese soldiers fought on, unaware that the war had ended.

One of these was Hiroo Onoda, who in 1944, as a 23-year-old second lieutenant, had been sent to Lubang Island, 75 miles south of the Philippines capital of Manila, to carry out guerrilla and intelligence duties. His orders were to carry on fighting even if his unit was destroyed. And Lieutenant Onoda did just that. He carried on fighting World War Two for the next 29 years.

Lieutenant Onoda.

THE WORLD'S GREATEST MISTAKES

After the war's end, leaflets were dropped by plane announcing Japan's surrender. They were signed by Onoda's chief of staff. The lieutenant picked up several of them, but dismissed them as American propaganda.

Over the years, the world changed drastically. The Iron Curtain split Europe in two. The first man journeyed into space. Japan once again grew prosperous, now a staunch ally of the United States.

But Onoda continued with his lonely war, carefully conserving his dwindling ammunition. He lived on bananas and coconuts, with the occasional snared jungle bird or stolen cow as a welcome luxury.

During his first few years in the jungle, Onoda was in touch with other isolated Japanese guerrillas. But, one by one, his comrades 'surrendered' or died, some of them by committing suicide. Finally, he was alone – one man surrounded by illusory enemies whom he attempted to shoot on sight.

He kept switching hideouts to avoid detection, sniping at the islanders, stealing cattle, burning crops. Police and search parties sent from Japan to try to make him surrender were met with bullets.

Onoda made sandals from woven straw and bits of old tyres held together with string and wooden pegs. When his clothes rotted, he patched them with tent canvas, using a piece of wire as a needle and plant fibre as thread. He built shelters of branches, bamboo, vines and leaves, but never dared stay for too long in one place.

Hunger was a permanent part of his life, and he was plagued by giant tropical ants, bees, centipedes, scorpions and snakes. To make fire, he rubbed together two pieces of split bamboo prepared with a mixture of coconut fibre and gunpowder from old bullets.

Friends, relatives and old comrades visited the island to tell him the war was over, and often he saw them and heard them calling to him through loudspeakers. From high ground, he could see the twinkling lights of the towns below. And he spotted luxury liners ablaze with lights out to sea. But he never once doubted that the war was still going on.

Then, in 1974 – 30 years after he first landed on Lubang – he stumbled across a Japanese student on a camping holiday. Onoda was about to shoot the young man, Norio Suzuki. But, fortunately, Suzuki had read all about the fugitive and quickly said: 'Onoda-san, the Emperor and the people of Japan are worried about you.'

Onoda said he would accept orders to lay down his arms only from his commanding officer, former Major Yoshimi Taniguchi. Now a bookseller, Taniguchi was flown to Lubang to meet a still-suspicious Onoda.

As soon as the tattered figure recognised Taniguchi, he snapped to attention and shouted: 'Lieutenant Onoda reporting for duty, sir!'

So, at 3 p.m. on March 10, 1974, Lieutenant Onoda at last stopped fighting

World War Two. It was his 52nd birthday.

Onoda was pardoned for his misdeeds in the Philippines by President Marcos. He went home and saw again his aged parents, who showed him the tombstone they had ordered for him at a time when they believed he had died in the jungle.

Onoda was greeted as a hero, and became famous around the world. But he could not stand the adulation. The man who had fought on alone for Japan decided to emigrate to Brazil.

After half a lifetime of war, he just wanted to find some peace.

The Kamikaze pilot who missed the boat

Haruo Hirota is alive today only because he made the biggest blunder of his life – and became part of military history.

His greatest wish was to die in battle as a kamikaze pilot. But it was not to be, and Hirota is believed to be the only Japanese kamikaze pilot to survive a mission.

In April, 1945, he climbed into his explosives-packed glider, slung under a bomber. Nineteen-year-old Hirota's suicidal mission was to steer the glider on to an American aircraft carrier.

All went to plan until the bomber above him was hit by American fighter planes. Hirota released his deadly glider and guided it towards the nearest big American ship. But instead of landing on the ship, Hirota missed his target, and the glider survived a hail of bullets and crashed into the sea.

Hirota, who had not achieved his ambition to die in battle, was full of shame for having blundered.

'I almost made it to the ship,' he explained, 'but suddenly I found myself under water. I had to be rescued by American sailors.'

After the war, Hirota married, had two children and settled down as a chef – in Washington D.C.